STANDING ON FAITH TOGETHER

In A Post-Pandemic World

Kathleen Zacca

Dedication

To every single person that reads this book: I've prayed for you many times, and I believe this is just the beginning. I dream of Christians standing on faith together as we watch God move like we've never seen or experienced before. My prayer is that you'll join the movement. We are stronger together. If you want to know *how* we're going to change the world…this book was written for you.

Table of Contents:

Introduction

The Coronavirus Pandemic of 2020 has brought fear, division, panic, uncertainty, and financial disaster unlike anything I've ever seen in my lifetime. There are so many questions that no one seems to have the answers to. Will our children ever go back to school without worrying about coronavirus? Will our economy recover from this? Will anything ever be the same again? There is too much information the media is throwing at us, which makes it difficult to figure out what is true versus what isn't. The news is flooded with everything that has to do with coronavirus, but there are many other scary things going on that are not being discussed as much in public. Things like sex-trafficking rings, rampant alcohol and prescription drug use, the violence among the homeless, children that are suffering abuse from the hands of their parents who are forced to stay home, and so much more. Our country seems more divided than it's ever been, and many of us are wondering how it got this bad.

Although coronavirus brought the entire world to a standstill, Covid-19 isn't the real problem we face. It goes much deeper than that. The bigger virus is that our hearts and minds are turned away from the things of God. This produces a lack of faith. I picture a concrete wall divider, and on one side is salvation, riches beyond our imagination, peace, love, joy, and eternity. On the other side of the wall is the world and all the enticing things it offers – sin, greed, lust, selfish desires, and more. So many people are sitting on top of that wall with their backs to the things God has for them while facing the world with excitement in their eyes. They haven't fully embraced the world because they don't want to disappoint God, yet the world is calling out to them. Many of those people will dive into that world, never looking back. There are also the ones that jumped off that wall long ago, and they think it's too late for them. How do we reach all those people? It's the million-dollar question, and it's the reason I wrote this book.

If we are to make a difference in this world, we must address the absence of faith in ourselves. In order to address this issue, we must first understand what faith is and why it's so important to God. Our faith in God can be powerful, because it moves Him.

Faith starts out as a tiny little seed, and it must be watered properly for it to grow. I'll take you through that process in the pages of this book. If the body of Christ grasps how important *our* faith is to God, boy oh boy – we'll see miracles beyond our wildest imagination.

I challenge you to read this book even if you have a good understanding of what faith is. Because after you read it, my hope and expectations are that you'll join me as we stand up and fight the enemy that is loose here on earth. The devil does his best to instill fear in each of us to keep us silent and our faith small. Not anymore. The body of Christ will unite, and our voices will be heard all around the world. As we unite and stand on faith together and as our voices grow louder, God will see and hear the cries of His people, and He'll show up in a mighty way. Prayers will be answered. The evil in this world will be brought to light and extinguished. Miracles will be manifested all around the world. The media will have a hard time explaining these miracles, because many will not understand what is happening – but we will understand. People will turn away from sin and worship God – our Creator. Victory after victory and testimony after testimony will be celebrated and heard everywhere. I'm about to break out in a praise-dance just writing these words. I can't wait to see what God is going to do. Our time is now.

In a world filled with billions of people, so many don't have a clue who God is. Some have been hurt so deeply that they don't want to try and understand why God would allow the things that hurt them to happen. So, they choose to walk away from anything that has to do with Him. There are also the ones that are playing tug-of-war with God and the devil. They go to church on Sundays, but live in sin during the week. There's no judgment here – I've been in all these categories. It took me longer than it should have to get me where I'm at now, and I'm grateful to God for not giving up on me. I've been through the fire; my faith has been tested time and time again, and I've made the decision to serve God with everything I am.

Since I made that decision, God has opened my eyes to faith and what it means to Him. It's so much more than just a word. My hope is that you'll fully understand its meaning after reading this book. If you're one of those people sitting on top of that concrete wall, or even if you're fully living in the world, I have insurmountable faith that you'll reconsider your choices after you read this book and see faith through the eyes of God. It's deep, and it's personal. My life changed forever after I made the decision to choose Him over what the world has to offer. I've spent the last twenty-one years seeking God and all His promises. He hasn't let me down even once. He's been through the worst days of my life with me, and I've found a peace that surpasses all understanding. I so desperately want that for you, too.

Christians, we are the body of Christ. We have power and authority in the name of Jesus. We are one in Christ; we are in unity. It's time for us to assert our power for the good of those who don't know the peace of God. It's time for us to expose the evil in this world. We have a voice, and the enemy cannot stand against the word of God. That is our weapon – our voices must be heard for the enemy to flee. The more we are silent, the more ground the enemy takes from us. We can no longer wait for someone else to do something – Jesus is coming back, we know this.

I believe a revival is coming. Do you feel it? That is the Holy Spirit in each of us preparing us for what's to come. The enemy wants to silence us by placing fear and rejection in our hearts and minds. We will be persecuted, just as Jesus was, but it shouldn't stop us because it didn't stop Him. We can't let the enemy win in this area. We must take ground now before it's too late. There are people waiting for us to help them turn away from sin. What God has placed in you is there for a reason. I encourage you to mount up and join Christians all around the world. Let's start a *movement* that will be unstoppable. I invite you to *Stand on Faith Together* with all of us and watch God perform miracle after miracle through our faith and unity. To God be the glory forever and ever. Amen!

CHAPTER ONE

How do we stand on faith together in a post-pandemic world? We boldly come together as the body of Christ. We face our fears and trust that God will do for us just as He did for the Israelites many years ago. I don't know if things will ever be the same, and maybe that's a good thing. What I do know is that we serve a mighty God who isn't scared of anything. We need change, we need Jesus, and we need to stand together so God can show us the power *we* have through our faith and obedience to Him. He's ready to show all of us exactly what He's capable of. If I were the devil, I'd be shaking in my boots.

When I began praying about writing this book, God showed me the tree of living water. He showed me that this tree represents the foundation of what our faith should look like.

In Jeremiah 17:7-8, the Lord says:

> *"But blessed is the one who trusts in the Lord, whose confidence is in him. They will be like a tree planted by the water that sends out its roots by the stream. It does not fear when heat comes; its leaves are always green. It has no worries in a year of drought and never fails to bear fruit."*

This verse is powerful. If our faith is in the One who created us, we shouldn't fear anything that tries to destroy us. Not even a pandemic. God is saying that if we put our trust in Him, we don't have to worry about anything. *No worries.*

The tree significantly relates to faith for many reasons. A tree must be rooted firmly in the ground for it to grow to its great height. My faith must be firmly rooted in God for it to grow and mature. As a tree begins to grow, it will start producing leaves. As my faith grows, I'll also start producing new things. My heart will begin to change, and instead of continuing in my old ways, I will begin to see things differently, and I'll have a strong desire to grow even more. Eventually, a tree grows into full maturity and it produces good fruit. As I mature in my faith, I also will produce good fruit for others around me. They will see God in me and learn about God and His kingdom.

The most important part of this process is supplying the tree with water for it to grow. Water is crucial for its growth. The most important part of growing our faith is reading the Bible. We can't grow without it. As we read His word, our roots are planted deeper and stronger in God. We are *watering* our faith. This is important because when the enemy attacks you (and he will), you'll need the word of God in your heart to deflect his attacks. If you don't have the weapons needed to fend off these attacks, you'll lose the battle, and sin will follow.

I've experienced being in a place of drought; I know what it's like to wonder where my next meal is going to come from. When my husband and I lost our business in 2009, we were scared. I didn't know how we were going to survive. After we exhausted all our savings, I lost hope. We began to run out of food, and I had to stand in lines at food banks for my family. I had to ask for help from my church and family to pay for our utility bills multiple times. This went on for almost five years. I begged God for help. My faith was weak, and at times it was non-existent. I didn't understand why we were suffering. It was painful, but even though my faith wavered, I didn't give up. By the grace of God, He provided just enough for my family to eat every day.

It was during that dark time that my faith began to grow. We survived that storm, and when I look back on it now, I can see what God did for my family. He was there, guiding and teaching me so many wonderful things that got me to where I am now: writing a book about faith. I have a heart for people that struggle with their faith because I've been there. I know the pain and I want to encourage others to push through it.

The tree is a symbol of mature faith. It symbolizes strength, depth, growth, healing, beauty, unity, and so much more. The tree of living water is referenced several times in the Bible. It's important for us to understand why God keeps referring to it. It's in Him that we can live our life to the fullest. It's in Him that we find peace and joy. It's in Him that we find a love that cannot be compared to anything else here on earth. Where His river flows, life is flourishing.

Connected to the Tree of Life

When a seed is planted, it begins to grow. The roots take hold in the dirt beneath the surface and spread to keep it firmly in place. Eventually, a sprout comes up from the ground. This is the first sign of hope for a tree. It has a lot of potential at this stage. Will it grow upward to be more than twenty feet tall? How wide will it be? What kind of leaves will it have? What kind of fruit will it bear?

The environment the tree is planted in will determine how it grows. The same goes for my faith. If I don't surround myself with what I need to grow my faith, it will never reach its potential.

The next stage is the sapling. Leaves start to grow, and the tree continues to grow taller. Branches begin reaching out from the tree. The sapling is well on its way to full maturity. God is so amazing in how he enlightens His children to see things the way He meant for them to be.

As I picture a tree growing from a seed to maturity, it becomes even clearer that my faith is very important to God. Just as a seed begins to grow and flourish, God wants the same thing to happen with our faith.

The final stage of a tree is maturity. A tree has many branches and leaves. At this stage, it's fully capable of bearing fruit, and it provides so many good things. At this point in my faith, I'm able to do the same for others.

Each growth stage is important. I can't skip any stage to become mature in my faith. If I tried to skip any of them, I would only be short-changing myself. I needed each trial and tribulation to become stronger. My experiences have shaped who I am today – a strong woman of faith. God will do the same for you. Hang in there – God will take care of all the details.

The Tree of Living Water

Faith is important to God for many reasons that I'll get into throughout this book, but I want to start by telling you that *our* faith matters. This is because *we* are connected to the tree of life. We are intertwined with each other; woven in and out and around one another all over the world. We are the branches on the tree, and we are unified together in Christ. It's our job to bear fruit for God's kingdom. It's much easier if we do this together instead of on our own.

In Ezekiel chapter 47, God showed Ezekiel a vision of a river flowing from the temple of God. This water flows out of the south side of the temple. It starts out ankle-deep, then knee-deep, moving to waist-deep. From there, the water was deep enough to swim in. In his vision, an angel from Heaven was guiding Ezekiel through the water, and once the water was over his head, the angel took Ezekiel back to the bank of the river. From here, I'll repeat the words in Ezekiel:

> *"When I arrived there, I saw a great number of trees on each side of the river. He said to me, 'This water flows toward the eastern region and goes down into the Arabah, where it enters the Dead Sea. When it empties into the sea, the salty water becomes fresh. Swarms of living creatures will live wherever the river flows.*

There will be large numbers of fish, because this water flows there and makes the saltwater fresh; so where the river flows everything will live. Fishermen will stand along the shore; from En Gedi to En Eglaim there will be places for spreading nets. The fish will be of many kinds – like the fish of the Mediterranean Sea. But the swamps and marshes will not become fresh; they will be left for salt. Fruit trees of all kinds will grow on both banks of the river. Their leaves will not wither, nor will their fruit fail. Every month they will bear fruit, because the water from the sanctuary flows to them. Their fruit will serve for food and their leaves for healing.'" (Ezekiel 47:7-12)

The Dead Sea has almost ten times the amount of salt that our oceans do. Because of this, nothing can live in its waters. In Ezekiel's vision, when the water that flows from the temple touches the water in the Dead Sea, there is life. Wow!

The saltwater becomes fresh. Fruit trees are growing along the river, providing abundant fruit for many to enjoy. The trees will continue to produce fruit because they are receiving water from the temple of God. The leaves of these trees will be used for healing. Just as the water from the temple of God touched the Dead Sea and cause fish to *live* in that water where the river is flowing, God's Holy Spirit does the same to humans – it makes the dead in spirit come alive. Amazing!

The river from the temple in Ezekiel's vision changed the salty Dead Sea into a sea of life. What does this mean? The power of God transforms death into life. The dead in Spirit come to life!

The tree and water are symbolic here. God wants us to understand the importance of the tree. He wants the tree to grow to a mature state to produce fruit. He wants the same for us and our faith. In Ezekiel's vision, God provided the water for the trees to grow where there was a dead wasteland. From a small seed to maturity, He'll provide all that we need along the journey. We'll continue to learn and grow, helping others along the way.

The tree of living water is mentioned again in the book of Revelation. The apostle John was given a vision of things to come. In the last chapter in this book, John was shown a vision of the restoration of Eden:

"Then the angel showed me the river of the water of life, as clear as crystal, flowing from the throne of God and of the Lamb down the middle of the great street of the city. On each side of the river stood the tree of life, bearing twelve crops of fruit, yielding its fruit every month. And the leaves of the tree are for the healing of the nations." (Rev. 22:1-2)

The tree of life is significant to God. The water flows from the throne of God, and the tree of life stands on both sides of the river. Again, it says that these trees bear fruit, and the leaves of the tree are used for healing.

Let me give you another important scripture that will help tie all of this together. In John 15:5, Jesus is speaking to His disciples.

"I am the vine, you are the branches. If you remain in me and I in you, you will bear much fruit; apart from me you can do nothing."

I'm a branch of Christ Jesus and so are you. Picture a tree in your mind. The branches extend outward and upward. There are more branches growing from other branches, and all of them have leaves or fruit. The fruit feeds God's children, and the leaves are used for healing. The tree of living water provides nourishment and sustenance. God wants the same from His children. He wants us to produce good fruit that will help guide others to the tree of living water.

The tree of life represents Jesus. The branches on the tree are the ones who follow and believe in Him – you and me. This tree would not be productive without the water that comes from the throne of God or His temple. Thus, the tree of living water.

Why Does Our Faith Matter to God?

Our faith matters to God because He wants us to produce good fruit. We can endeavor to learn as much as we possibly can about God, and about what Jesus has done and will continue to do for us. But He doesn't want us to stop there. As Christians, we're connected to the tree of life, and we're not alone. There are many people connected to the *same* tree. We are in unity together. We are the body of Christ. When we pray in faith together, we are inviting the presence and the power of the Holy Spirit to surround us. The atmosphere is different when God's people pray and worship together.

As we pray together, our faith increases, because we believe God is going to do something miraculous. Also, when we pray together, we bond in fellowship and abandon our selfish desires while coming together in unity.

Here's an example: I'm at church around other people that are praying alongside me, and we're all seeking answers for healing, guidance, or wisdom. Because of my struggles, my faith is weak, and I'm not sure that God even cares about me. But as I'm praying with others, God begins bringing all of us in unity together – one body, one heart, one mind. My faith is strengthened with the body of Christ. He shows us together what we are seeking. When we pray together, we begin to desire God's purposes and not our own.

Unity is a side effect of God's people praying in faith together. There is wisdom, joy, peace, and laughter in unity. We need to understand we are connected to the tree of living water, together – and it's when we are in unity together that God will show up mightily and move on our behalf. In 2 Chronicles 7:13-14 the Lord said:

> *"…if my people, who are called by my name, will humble themselves and pray and seek my face and turn from their wicked ways, then I will hear from heaven, and I will forgive their sin and will heal their land."*

How many times have we heard this verse? What is it going to take for us to actually *do* this? When tragedy, trials, or tribulations come upon us, we need to join together and pray in faith for God to move mountains for His people. He's done it before, and He'll do it again. We have a worldwide pandemic on our hands – this is the perfect opportunity for us to seek God.

In the verse above, God clearly states what He'll do, but we must do our part. As the body of Christ or branches of the tree of living water, we are connected to the One that knows all things. And as we pray in faith together, He will move mountains. He will protect us from the enemy of this world. He will heal our brokenness. He will bring unity where there is division. He will bring light to the darkness. He will turn our sorrow into joy. We need His guidance during the unprecedented time we are experiencing in today's world. We are better, stronger, and smarter when we stand on faith together. We could change the world. Let's do this – together.

Importance of Faith

Have you ever felt unsettled by events happening around you? When things happen that are beyond my control, it rattles me, leaving me feeling unsure, and sometimes lost. It could be something as simple as my job duties changing or something as devastating as a death in my family from a serious world pandemic.

Changes can be hard. Faith is the only way I know how to cope with anything that has me feeling unsettled, confused, hurt, angry, or lost. I remind myself that God isn't surprised by any event happening around me. He knew my husband and I were going to lose our business when the economic crisis happened. He knew all the struggles we were going to go through from the result of that loss. I grew stronger in my faith during this difficult time.

He knew my mother was going home to heaven. He knew I wasn't prepared for it. My faith carried me through that devastating loss. He also knew about the coronavirus world pandemic of 2020. He knew the fear I would experience, not knowing how this was going to affect my family and the entire world. During quarantine, I asked God what I could do to help others. He doesn't waste any season. The time of isolation helped me take time to reflect on my life and write this book.

Faith has brought me through every single surprising, unsettling event that has come upon me. I choose faith because God has never failed me. Through my faith, God has shown me Himself: the way He loves me. The way He forgives and extends grace and mercy. His incomparable peace. His amazing wisdom. How to honor Him through worship and thankfulness. His integrity and His holiness. All these things are a part of who He is. I want to know more about Him; I want to be more like Him. I strive to accomplish this daily through my faith in Him.

Faith is one of the most important decisions you will ever make. Once you put your faith in God, everything in your life will change. This is more than the salvation decision. It is the choice to allow him to be the Lord. Faith is trusting that His way will always be better than my way.

The journey I've been on since I made that decision has been amazing. Every single day, I prayed for God to change me, and I asked for Him to show me what my purpose was. Day by day, He answered those prayers, and I'm thankful for all that He's done for me and my family. I now rely on my faith in every thought that enters my mind and every decision I make. I've learned to filter everything through my faith. No matter what comes up in my life, I know God has a plan for me, my husband, and our family. My past no longer matters, because my sins have been forgiven by my most important fan – God. He has a plan for you and your family, too. He wants us to succeed in all that we do.

Faith brought me from the deepest pits to His glorious light. Faith is the reason I get up every single morning. My faith in Him is personal, and it carries me through all the good and bad that breezes through my life. I've been on the verge of giving up on faith several times, because let's be honest – life is hard. But God never gave up on me. It's because He's been through all my trials and tribulations with me, always encouraging and loving, that I choose to continue my faith journey. I've come out stronger on the other side of each trial, and I remain humble and grateful to the One that loves me enough to extend His infinite love, grace, and mercy to a plain ol' country girl like me.

I have a deep love for Jesus, my Savior. He's my knight in shining armor. He's my rock. He's my comforter when I need Him the most. He forgives me when I don't deserve it. He pushes me to move forward when I don't think I'm good enough. He reminds me that I'm a daughter of the King, and the benefits that come from being His. He laughs and cries with me. He encourages me when I'm struggling. He loves me even when I make foolish mistakes. He's a good, good Father. I could continue praising Him, but you get the point. He's amazing.

Our faith is *personal* to God. Your experiences of faith will be different than mine. He knows better than anyone here on earth what brings joy and sorrow to your heart. He will laugh with you and bring you comfort when needed. Trust in Him.

God explains what faith is in Hebrews 11:1:

"Now faith is being sure of what we hope for and certain of what we do not see."

It has so much meaning and depth, and it has carried me through many desperate times. It's difficult to be sure in what I hope for if I can't see it, but after walking in faith, I've seen the unexplainable. I call them God moments. I pray, I ask, and I have faith that God will take care of it. I leave it there and trust God to hear me. It may not happen immediately, but He always takes care of my prayers and my heart.

What God moments have you seen or experienced in your own life? I want you to write those God moments down. Keep them close to your heart, because someone somewhere needs to hear what you've seen and experienced with Him.

Faith is the bridge between you and God. When your landscape begins to change before your eyes, do you choose to walk that bridge with trust, even though you don't know what's going to happen? Or do you step off the bridge and try to figure it out on your own? I've done both. With confidence, I can say that every time I tried on my own, I failed. When I chose to stay on the bridge of faith, I was scared, but every time I have chosen faith, God has miraculously brought me through it better and stronger. Sometimes it's not how I imagined it, but I trust that His way is better, and I have faith that He knows what's best for me. He'll do the same for you.

Because I have faith in God, the devil does everything within his power to place doubt in my heart and mind. The devil knows my weaknesses, and he pursues those weaknesses with everything he's got. One of the many tools he uses is fear. When fear comes, we must trust in the One who tells us fear is a liar. We should not listen to the whispers of the enemy trying to convince us that we're not good enough, smart enough, or confident enough to speak God's truth. When fear rears its ugly head, we must put it back in its place. We are children of God; a son or daughter of the King, and He will fight our battles with the enemy. We must have faith that He will protect us and keep us moving forward to accomplish the assignment He has for each of us.

Faith is important, because without it, we couldn't have a relationship with God. Without it, we wouldn't have a deep, abiding love with Jesus, our Savior. It's through our faith that God answers our prayers and performs miracles. Faith is the difference between Heaven and Hell. I encourage and implore you to ask God how your faith is today and allow Him to show you how much your faith means to Him.

Faith Pleases God

God knows it isn't easy to believe in something I can't see. I'm a visual person, so for me – seeing is believing. I don't see God in the flesh, but I know He exists because I pursue a relationship with Him. It didn't happen overnight. It took time to build a strong relationship with Him, just as it did with my husband. My relationship with God consists of faith, trust, love, honor, respect, and spending time praying to and talking with Him. According to Hebrews 11:6, my faith pleases God; it brings Him joy, and He rewards the ones who seek Him. Because of my faith, I have high expectations of good things to come. God sees my desires, and He wants to give me these things through my faith and obedience to Him.

Faith can't be explained away by reason. It's rooted deep in my heart and spirit. It lives where my deepest desires reside. It's this feeling of knowing that things will get better, even though I can't see it. I've been through enough trials and tribulations in my life to know that God always has a higher purpose for every struggle I go through. God wants me to learn and become better through each of these trials. He teaches me new things. He shows me new ways to do things – better ways, than I could ever do on my own. The more I put my faith and trust in God, the stronger I become. When something comes up in my life that rattles me, my first words are always, "God, I need You." He immediately responds, *I'm here. I'm with you.* Peace enters my heart and fear leaves. I know He'll get me through it, because He has every single time.

Knowing that my faith pleases God pushes me to dig deeper in its treasure. Where there is abundant faith, there is abundant treasure. I think about the blessing of my marriage and the trust and faith my husband and I have in each other. It pleases me to know that my husband can trust me, and he has faith in me to always treat him with the respect he deserves. My children have faith in me that I will be there for them when they need me. It brings me great joy to know that they feel safe and happy when they are with me and their dad. This faith and trust are tangible to my family. They can see and touch me. They have no doubts that I'm here for them, always. How much more is God pleased with my faith in Him because I can't see or touch Him in the flesh? This is intimacy that goes far beyond the desires of my flesh. It's deeply personal and profound. My heart craves to know Him.

Reading the Bible helps me learn more about my Father. Praying and talking to Him brings me closer to Him. He has only good intentions for me. He wants me to succeed in all that I do. The most beautiful thing about my faith is it fills God with joy, and He wants to shower me with His love and blessings. What more could I ask for? He will fulfill my every need and desire because of my faith in Him.

When I decided to follow Jesus, this angered the enemy of my soul. He continues to try and convince me that I'm not good enough to do what God has called me to do. He distracts me from my purpose; he whispers negative thoughts, and when I'm having a rough day, it's hard to always say and do the right thing. He might fool me for a minute, but it doesn't take me long to figure out what he's trying to do. I let the devil know I will not tolerate him interfering in my life. I simply start praying for God to rescue me from any negative, evil thoughts. God always answers that prayer.

It's important for me to be intentional with my faith. I know it's important to God, and I know it angers the devil. The more my faith builds, the harder the enemy tries to stop me from reaching my full potential. I want to teach others the importance of faith and the blessings that will come from growing their faith in God. In the Bible, there are many stories about faith and what God has done through that faith. I'll start with one from the Old Testament. His name was Job.

Job – A Man of Great Faith

Job was a man that had strong faith in God, and this got the attention of the devil. Job was blessed with money, land, a good family, and he was highly respected by his friends. The devil tried to convince God the only reason Job's faith was so strong was because God had blessed him mightily. The devil claimed that if all these things were taken away from Job, he knew that Job would curse God.

The devil underestimated Job and his faith. God took away all the things Job loved: his children, livestock, money, friends, and his health. Things became so bad that his wife even tried to convince him to curse God and die.

Job was devastated, but he remained faithful through it all. He had an intimate relationship with God, and although He didn't understand why his whole life had been turned upside down, he refused to curse God. Because he remained faithful, God restored his health, and multiplied Job's family and his worldly possessions even greater than they were before. His faith carried him through one of the worst things that ever happened to him, and God blessed the latter part of Job's life more than the first.

When facing tragedy, I can't always say that my faith didn't waver. I've questioned God multiple times. It's painful and heartbreaking going through something difficult, but I've come through those storms each time with stronger faith. I know it has propelled me to discover my true purpose in life. I can only imagine how Job felt when everything was taken away from him. His stress and anxiety had to be at a level that should have thrown him into a deep depression. He was clearly in anguish, but he wouldn't speak against God. His faith triumphed over the fear, stress, and anxiety that comes from devastation. What an amazing display of a man in right standing with God!

When I passionately pursue a relationship with God, He shows me the importance of faith. By listening to His words of wisdom, faith lives in my heart when my mind tells me it isn't possible. Faith is important to God because He created each one of us, and He doesn't want us to spend eternity apart from Him. It is through our faith that we can and will find solutions to all the problems we have in life. Our faith takes us to the author of all life, and He has the answers we're seeking. Our faith is precious to our Creator.

Faith Is Personal and Intimate

Before I move on, I want to talk about how personal and intimate faith is. The reason it's so personal is because no one knows us like God knows us. My husband is a close second, but he doesn't know my thoughts or everything that I do when I'm away from him. God, on the other hand, knows *all* these things, and He still loves me.

Faith is knowing that God sees all my mistakes and doesn't give up on me. He chastises, as a father should, and encourages me to do better. Faith is knowing He's proud of me when I do the right thing. No words need to be spoken; I just know my heavenly Father is pleased with me. Faith is trusting that God knew what was going to happen before my world got turned upside down, and it's also knowing that He will guide and direct me through it. Faith is trusting God during a pandemic that has affected millions of people all around the world, and knowing there will be good things that come from this tribulation. Faith is trusting that God has a better way than the way I thought it was supposed to be. It means trusting in Him even though I see the opposite of what I'm praying for. Faith is intimate because I know I'm different than other people – God created each person uniquely – and He knows all my quirky thoughts and ways. He gets me like no one else – that is intimacy. Now that I have a close, personal relationship with Him, I don't have to hide anything. I can be myself with Him, and it's one of the greatest feelings to know that I can depend on Him in every situation.

I know that when I'm hurting, I can go to Him, and He'll be there to comfort me. If I didn't have faith, I couldn't get that all-encompassing feeling of peace and love that I can only get from God. No words need to be spoken because my God knows my every thought. He knows my joy and my sadness. He knows my failures and my victories. He knows what I struggle with; He understands me. My faith is personal, private, and special, and He knows how to make me feel loved and cherished. My relationship with Him is the most important relationship in my life. It helps me love my husband more completely. It helps me be a better mother to my children. It allows me to be the best version of myself, which is what everyone around me deserves. He challenges and encourages me when I want to give up, and He picks me up when I fall. He is the best part of me, and He always will be. I will never underestimate the power that faith has had in my life. It changed me forever, and I'm completely humble and grateful to God for showing me the way.

Intimacy allows God full access to my heart. His word says:

"The Lord does not look at the things people look at. People look at the outward appearance, but the Lord looks at the heart." (1 Samuel 16:7).

My heart is where I feel His love and peace. It's also where I feel pain and rejection. Because I have allowed God full access to my heart, he knows my pain, rejection, fears, and He knows what makes me happy and how I love Him and other people. This intimacy permits God to heal me and chase away my fears. I feel His presence all around me when I pray, and He shows me His love – it's breathtaking. I couldn't experience any of this without my faith.

I want to fulfill all the plans He has for me, and I wouldn't be able to do that without complete and total trust in Him. The assignment He has for me is my personal assignment. He created me to carry out a very specific task. My current assignment is to write a book for you about the importance of faith and what it means to God, and to encourage Christians to unite and *stand on faith together*. When this happens, God will see and hear from Heaven, and He will move mightily here on earth. As I continue to pray about this vision God gave me, I get excited about what He's going to do. It's going to be unlike anything we've ever seen or experienced. We're going to unite and push the enemy back. We will bring God's light to the darkest places. Get ready!

God has a specific assignment for you, too. Keep praying and have faith. When I'm working on what God wants me to do, I'm at peace. I find so much joy in my work. A good example of someone that had a very specific assignment in the Bible is Noah.

Noah's Assignment

Noah lived in a time when the entire world was corrupt. Picture this for a moment – there was no hope, only evil and sin. We live in a corrupt world today, but there is hope and faith everywhere. Even though we hear of tragedies happening, we also hear the many good things that take place all around us. In Noah's time, that wasn't the case. Everyone was sinning and living as though nothing mattered. Evil demonic forces had taken over the earth. Unrighteousness was prevalent everywhere. Every thought that came from the people living in that time was evil and wicked.

A lot of life happened between the generations of the first man, Adam, and Noah. Satan ruled earth as his dominion, and he had only one purpose in mind – to destroy all that God had created. The descendants of Adam and Eve never knew what it was like to live in peace and harmony. The sins of mankind multiplied, and during this time, there wasn't a justice system set up. People did as they pleased with no worry of being punished for their actions. This grieved God, and He had to put a stop to it.

"The Lord saw how great man's wickedness on the earth had become, and that every inclination of the thoughts of his heart was only evil all the time. The Lord was grieved that he had made man on the earth and his heart was filled with pain." (Genesis 6:5)

Noah was the tenth descendant of Adam, and he was the only one on earth that found grace in God's eyes. He was surrounded by people that didn't want anything to do with God. There was something different about him. His lifestyle wasn't the same as the rest of the world. Genesis 6:9 says that Noah was righteous, had faith, and walked with God. He was a contrast to the people living during that time, and because of this, Noah found favor in God's eyes.

God had a very specific mission for Noah and his family. He asked Noah to build an ark big enough to house Noah, his family, and at least two of every animal God had created. He gave Noah the exact measurements and the details of what supplies he would need to build it. This wouldn't be an easy task, and it would take decades to build.

Pause here for a moment and think about this. Noah was instructed to build a large ship that would carry all that God was asking for. He was to take two of every creature God created. How was Noah going to get these animals onto the ark? How were they going to *live* together on this ark? How were they going to feed these animals? What were Noah and his family going to eat? As a woman, I'm thinking of all the details that would go into something like this. What do I need to pack? How much food and water do I need to bring on this massive ship? What about my vegetable garden? How long would this trip last? I would have questioned Noah. "Honey, are you sure this is what God asked you to do?"

It just doesn't seem possible until you visit the Ark Encounter in Grant County, Kentucky. The centerpiece of the park is a large representation of **Noah's Ark,** based on the Genesis flood narrative contained in the Bible. It is incredible that you can tour a full-scale replica of Noah's ark. But Noah did not have that luxury of seeing the vision in the natural before he built it. He had to trust God's plan.

Noah was strong in his faith, and in Genesis 6:22 it says, *"Noah did everything just as God commanded him."*

Noah built the ark, and when he was six hundred years old, God told him to gather his family and get on the ark. He sent all the animals to Noah, and they boarded the ark two at a time. God commanded the animals, and they obeyed. It's amazing to think about all the things that had to take place for this venture to happen. What seems too hard for us is a simple task for God. It's why our faith is so important – we simply can't do what God can and will do for His children.

When Noah, his family, and all the animals were on the ark, God sent the rain. It rained for forty days, and the entire earth flooded, killing every animal and human that was on dry land. This was a sin pandemic of the greatest magnitude. The death toll was staggering. Our current coronavirus death rates are less than .001% of the population. Can you imagine if you were living in Noah's time? That number would be the SURVIVAL rate!

Noah and his family were quarantined on the ark for an entire year. I think we can relate to that family now more than ever before. It doesn't say how Noah and his family did while on the ark. Were they happy? Were they frustrated? Did they complain about the confinement? Did they get on each other's nerves? What did they do without an ipad?

Did they know what to expect once their journey was complete? They had to be grieving for the loss of humans and animals. It was a tragedy they had never experienced before, and one that no one will ever have to go through, because as soon as God told them it was safe to come out of the ark, He promised He would never again destroy all living creatures. He made a covenant with Noah and all his descendants, declaring His promise. The sign for this covenant is the rainbow. When I see a rainbow in the sky, it reminds me that this covenant still stands today.

When this pandemic is over, what are we going to be left with? How different will our world be? Right now, things aren't looking so great. The enemy is here – roaming and roaring – looking for people to devour and destroy. We are divided, and in some areas, we seem to be falling completely apart. The good news is, we *can* do something about it – and it starts with us uniting in faith. God is waiting for us to unite and stand up to the enemy. We can do it. I believe we *will* do it.

Noah's faith changed the course of the entire world. If Noah didn't have faith, none of us would be here today. This story blesses me in so many ways. What effect is my faith having on the people around me? What impact will my faith leave for others here on earth? I want my children's faith to be strong, and I want them to teach the same thing to my grandchildren. The best gift I could ever give my children is teaching them about faith. The rest is in God's capable hands. He will show each of them what they are called and qualified for.

Noah is a great example of someone that can have strong faith even though sin was all around him. I'm sure he prayed for some of the people that he knew, just as I pray for my friends and family. I know it was hard for him because it's still hard today. The good news is that God will reward my faith just as He rewarded Noah and his family. We exist today because Noah was a righteous, faithful man, and because God had mercy on mankind. Noah's faith encourages me to continue my journey of faith, and I want to encourage others as well.

When I look at the names in the Bible, there were many that were faithful. I have read about Moses, Abraham, Esther, Nehemiah, David, Jacob, Joseph, Peter, Paul, and so many more. They weren't perfect, but each of them were called to carry out an assignment for God.

Moses was called to get God's people out of Egypt. It wasn't an easy task, and it took him forty years to do it – but by faith and with the help of God, he did it. Joseph was left for dead by his brothers, and later sent to prison. His faith brought him out of prison to Pharaoh's second in command. God gave Joseph wisdom that saved all of Egypt during a seven-year famine.

Every story in the Bible required faith in God to get them through it. Where there was faith, there was God. That is a message for us even today. If we have faith to overcome this pandemic we are in, I believe God will vanquish it. Everything we go through requires our faith. We can't see nor do we understand all the things that are happening to or around us, but with faith, we know God sees all of it. Knowing that God doesn't want us to suffer and He loves us unconditionally helps us know that we're not alone. He will be with us through the storm because that's the kind of God He is.

The foundation of faith is talked about several times in the Bible. The Lord compares faith to a tree planted near the water. The comparison to a tree is astonishing because a tree goes through many different stages before it becomes a mature tree. My faith is the same way. I've gone through many stages to get where I'm at now. The process was slow, yet so fulfilling. In order for a tree to grow, it must be watered constantly. Without water, the tree will not survive. The same concept applies to our faith. If we want our faith to grow, we need to provide the key ingredient to move the process along to mature it. That key ingredient is God's word.

My favorite Bible verse is the one I mentioned earlier in this chapter. It is Hebrews 11:1:

"Now faith is being sure of what you hope for and certain of what you do not see."

It's my favorite verse because faith has changed my life. I'm sure of what I hope for, and I'm confident and certain of the things I don't see, because I know God sees all things. I have deep faith, love, and trust in God because He loves me unconditionally. What is your favorite Bible verse? If you haven't found one yet, ask Him to reveal one to you. Memorize it. Pray it back to Him often.

CHAPTER ONE: FAITH

Who is the most faithful person you know? How?

What is a Bible verse that means something to you? Why?

What is the one thing you could do to increase your faith?

CHAPTER TWO

Seeds rest in the cold. Winter brings freezing weather, and the days are long and dark. The grass turns brown, the flowers stop budding, and the leaves fall from the trees, leaving the landscape looking drab and barren. The atmosphere can feel lonely and depressing, unless you understand the season of rest and cold. Sometimes it feels like it will last forever.

Winter used to be my least favorite of all four seasons. I longed for the warmth of sunshine and the beauty of flowers in bloom. Even though winter brings on thoughts and feelings of stillness and quiet, I have learned to embrace it. The Bible says in Genesis 8:22 that –

"As long as the earth endures, seedtime and harvest, cold and heat, summer and winter, day and night will never cease."

Winter isn't going anywhere, and just like every other season, it has its purpose.

In winter, trees lie dormant. The tree stops actively growing. Winter is a time of rest here on earth. The top layers of soil freeze, but beneath the frozen soil it looks much different. Organic matter such as mulch, compost, and leaves help insulate the soil. It's like a blanket covering the ground, keeping everything safe and warm beneath the surface. Soil-dwelling animals burrow beneath the soil and live there until winter ends. The soil protects plant and tree roots from freezing. Everything slows down, and the busyness of life is paused for a time.

A tree knows different seasons. It disrobes in winter, and it rests – quietly waiting for the hyperactive season of spring. Just as seasons are important and necessary here on earth, they are the same for our spiritual lives. There is a time for new beginnings, growth, great harvest, and rest. I've discovered that I enter my winter seasons reluctantly, but I've also found that it's the time that I connect the most to God. He speaks to me in the quiet, cold, and desperate places in my heart. As I lean into His peace and love, He redirects my thoughts, and guides me to His path.

"He makes me lie down…he leads me beside quiet waters, he restores my soul." (Psalm 23)

Harsh winters surprise us. Have you ever been in a prolonged winter season that seemed like it would never end? I mentioned in the first chapter that my husband and I lost our business. We were flourishing before the economic crisis hit. It was like harvest season. We lived in our dream home and life seemed so easy during that time. I wasn't prepared for what was just around the corner – a long winter that completely changed our lives.

I had no idea at the time that it would last almost a decade. I was devastated to the point that I walked away from serving and attending my church. I didn't know the plans God had for me; beautiful plans that required a long winter season for me to change my heart to the things God wanted for me – things I've always desired but didn't know how to pursue. I was busy helping others in our church, helping my husband with our business, and raising our children. But God wanted to redirect my path and a winter season had me lying down.

I remember sitting in my prayer closet, begging Him to restore what my husband and I had lost. Now I'm so grateful for God and what He did for me during that time of isolation. He truly restored my soul. It changed my life for the better. I discovered my true purpose during that winter season, and I never would have if I had continued to walk the path I was on. If you're in a winter season, I want to encourage you to rest and to be led by God through it. He will show you the way.

I'm so amazed at how God set things up here on earth. There is so much depth and meaning to everything He creates. He created the seasons we experience here on earth, and it's a joy that we get to personally enjoy each of these seasons in our hearts, too. Only God has the timetable for the length of each season we go through. Winter is a time for digging in deeper with God. It's much-needed rest before the spring season comes – and it will come in God's perfect timing.

When desolation surrounds me, the only thing I have left is faith. I start with a small seed of faith and plant it into the depth of my heart. I continue to water it daily with living water – God's word. Now, I'm watching it grow into something beautiful that will provide fruit for generations. The same will happen for you.

If you've had a long winter season, write it down at the end of this chapter. I'd love to hear your story. Remember that God has a purpose for everything, and no matter what your story is – you are loved and cherished.

The Power of a Tiny Seed

Seeds can be tiny in relation to the size of the fruit, and they come in all shapes and sizes. When seeds are planted, they are desperate to grow. They have a coat of armor on the outside for protection until they arrive in a fertile environment. This coat serves as a barrier to fungi, heat, cold, or any other elements that may destroy it.

Just like a seed is protected by the flesh of the fruit, God protected the seed of faith that was planted in me at a young age. To know that God loved me during the time I made many mistakes is so special to me. If He didn't love me, He wouldn't have pursued me. His love is more than I can comprehend, and I'm so thankful for His persistence. He pursues each of His children with the same love and persistence.

There is a lot that goes on inside the seed before it finally breaks free and sprouts. Underneath the seed coat is a baby plant, or embryo. When the time is right and the seed is properly watered and cared for, it will sprout and begin to take root in the ground. When a seed finally sprouts, it's like a breath of fresh air that brings hope after a cold, hard winter.

The potential that one tiny seed has is astounding. It will grow into a large plant or tree that will produce fruit and other seeds for years to come. In Mark 13:31-32 Jesus said:

"The kingdom of heaven is like a mustard seed, which a man took and planted in his field. Though it is the smallest of all seeds, yet when it grows, it is the largest of the garden plants and becomes a tree, so that the birds come and perch in its branches."

A tiny seed planted in the ground has a bright future. Just like the tiny seed, my faith will grow into a large tree with many branches if gently nurtured with living water.

When I first became a Christian, my faith was as small as a mustard seed. The seed of faith was planted when I was a child, and it stayed just beneath the surface until I became an adult. My parents never went to church, but I went occasionally with friends. As I grew older, those church visits stayed with me. God was always in the back of my mind, and because I had some knowledge of Him, I considered myself a believer. I believed He existed, but I had never read the Bible, and the only experiences I'd had were when I attended church those few times as a child. The seed was there, waiting to be watered, but it had not sprouted. I always felt something tugging at my heart, but I didn't know what it was, so I ignored it for a long time.

When I was in my early twenties, my mom and stepdad started going to church, and they both got saved. It completely changed them. My stepdad was an alcoholic, and after he found Jesus, he never picked up another drink. My mom was so happy, and I could see the peace and joy on her face. It was enough to move me to start going to church. My husband and I attended church for several years, but there was still something missing. I didn't have the same experience that my parents did, so I was doubtful, and I began going less and less often. It wasn't until I was thirty-one years old that I had that life-changing experience with God.

Before it happened, I couldn't sleep most nights. I would wake up and hear voices around me – voices that instilled fear in me. It was dark, and I couldn't see anything, but I felt the presence of evil. I would try to sit up and I couldn't. It felt like I was being held down. I tried to speak so I could wake my husband up, and the sounds that came out of my mouth were not my own. It was an evil voice, and I was terrified. The only thing I knew to do at that point was to say the name of Jesus, so I did – over and over again. I felt the rage around me when I spoke His name, so I kept saying it until the evil presence was gone. This happened more times than I can count. I knew something was wrong, and I began to fear going to sleep. My husband slept soundly next to me every single time this happened. After several weeks of this, I called my mom and told her about it. My stepdad got on the phone and said he'd be at my house in an hour. He showed up and anointed my entire house with oil.

My stepdad told me he'd been praying for me and my family, and he knew I was being attacked spiritually. I wasn't sure what he meant at the time, but because I was so terrified of what had been happening to me, I was ready to do whatever it took to make it stop. My mom looked up different churches in the area, and she found a little church that I'd never heard of before.

We went the next day, and I'll never forget it. I accepted Jesus that day, and I walked down to the front of the church when the Pastor did an altar call. There were several people that accepted Jesus, and we were standing shoulder to shoulder. The Pastor came and talked to each one of us individually. When he stood in front of me, I was crying. He placed his hands on my shoulders and asked, "Do you accept Jesus as your Lord and Savior?"

I replied, "Yes."

He then said, "The demons that have been coming to you while you sleep will never come again. You'll no longer have to fear them. You've been set free by the power of the Holy Spirit. Do you understand?"

I nodded, because I couldn't speak at that point. I was in disbelief. How did he know what had been happening to me? A woman walked over to me and placed her hands on my arms. She spoke these words, "Don't ever forget what you're about to experience. I want you to always remember this moment." I still remember it vividly. There was such an intense look in her eyes.

Both the Pastor and this woman began praying for me, and what happened next is hard for me to describe. I felt something come out of my body. I couldn't see it, but I could feel it. I also felt an abundance of joy, peace, love, and overwhelming relief. I felt like a brand new person. I remember walking back to my husband and family with this huge smile on my face that must have stayed there for hours. To this day, those demons have never come to me again. I accepted Jesus and it changed my life. All of this started from a seed planted when I was just a child. I'll never underestimate the potential of a tiny seed.

The Beauty of Tragedy

When tragedy occurs, change happens within and around us. Everything that was normal before now seems foreign. It isn't a pleasant feeling, and it usually leaves one feeling fear of the unknown. The landscape has changed, and desolation is visible, with no hope of ever finding peace or happiness again. How do we survive trauma and tragedy? God's word says the ones who mourn are blessed, and He will comfort them (Matt. 5:4). He is with us when we're suffering. He is the light at the end of the dark tunnel. God already knows what is going to happen, and He is all around us when tragedy, trials, and tribulation come upon us.

The coronavirus world pandemic is a perfect example of tragedy changing the course of many of our lives. Coronavirus stopped everything all around the world. Many businesses closed for weeks. People were left without jobs or income. Fear settled in because the landscape changed. Simple errands like going to the grocery store were difficult because of fear of exposure to the virus. There was a shortage of food in the stores, and simple necessities such as toilet paper and baby formula were unavailable. Many people didn't have the funds to buy the things they needed. Schools and churches closed their doors. Everything shifted to digital platforms, and even schools went to viewing and learning online.

A new normal set in, and some embraced it, while others struggled with the many changes that took place during this time. This wasn't something anyone asked for, and we had little control over the things happening around us. This wasn't a war that had to be fought with guns, airplanes, bombs, and soldiers. This war brought doctors, nurses, truck drivers, and grocery workers to the forefront. They were our heroes during this unprecedented time. They were on the front lines, facing this virus every single day to protect and provide for each of us.

We became very familiar with old terms like "quarantine" and new ones like "social distancing." We had to isolate ourselves from family, friends, and co-workers. There was a frenzy of everyone buying masks to help prevent the spread of coronavirus. It was odd walking into a grocery store and seeing so many people wearing masks. Things changed and progressed quickly. It was an unfamiliar feeling to know that this pandemic affected the entire world. Everything felt smaller, and I felt more connected to people in other countries who were experiencing the same thing.

When forced to stay at home because of the fear of spreading the virus, family dynamics began to change. Homeschooling became the new normal for many parents. Parents spent more time with their children.

The chaos of life slowed down, and many people began to see this as a benefit during the pandemic. Spring cleaning and remodeling was taking place in many homes, and creative juices began to flow because people had time on their hands. What else could they do?

During this quiet time, I knew it was the right time to write this book. God began giving me details that sparked a fire deep within my heart, and I knew it wouldn't stop until I wrote it down. If God has been speaking to you, I encourage you to write it down at the end of this chapter. If God gave you the vision, He will provide a way to make it happen. Have faith.

Although many families were affected by this worldwide pandemic, a lot of good things came from it. There is so much division in our world today, and it's exhausting sometimes to watch and hear it on the news or social media every day. Coronavirus changed that for a short time. It was all the news outlets were talking about. It changed the momentum of everything we were used to seeing, hearing, or doing. It took the wind out of our sails, and everything came to a screeching stop. In a strange way, we were in unity, because even though it was out of our control, we were all in it together.

We had a new appreciation for people with essential jobs because they worked hard to keep all of us supplied with basic necessities. There were a lot of companies that had to change their dynamic to working from home. For some, it was an easy transition, but for others it wasn't. Restaurants closed their doors, and only some of them offered pick up service. Fast-food restaurants changed to drive-through only. It was a tragedy that no one had expected.

Tragedies are a very real part of life. They are horrific, and no one wants to experience the pain and change that comes from it. I've been through some of my own tragedies, and I remember thinking I just want it to end. It's during these times that I've questioned God the most. The lesson I've learned when tragedy strikes is to dig deeper into my faith in God. When I feel pain that is ripping my heart in half, He knows, and

He's the only One that can bring me the comfort I need. He's brought me through many things that I never would have been able to handle on my own.

Before the pandemic, my mother passed away. I was living in Austin, Texas, and she lived in east Texas. It was a little over four hours away. I knew she wasn't doing well, so I made the trip multiple times while she was ill. Several of these visits were to the hospital, while others were to her home. Even though I knew she wasn't doing well, I never thought it was getting close to her time to leave us. I had faith that she would get better, and we would go shopping again or enjoy one of my favorite meals she cooked for her family.

The last time I visited her before she passed was at home. She was still weak from her last hospital stay, so she needed help with simple things like getting out of the bed to take a shower. She was also on a special diet, so she wanted me to cook several meals that would last a week or two. After everything was checked off on her to-do list for me, I remember sitting on the bed with her, talking about silly things, but there were two things that stood out from that conversation. The first was she told me she didn't want to die because she wasn't ready to leave her family. I immediately told her that wasn't going to happen, because she was going to get better. She nodded and told me she wasn't so sure. My mom knew her time was close – I was in denial.

The second thing that stood out was she opened her wallet and showed me a little card that she had kept in her wallet for years. On the back there was a picture of an angel, and in my mother's handwriting it read simply, "To: Kathy, From: Mom." There was a poem on the front that said:

"May God grant you always… a sunbeam to warm you, a moonbeam to charm you, a sheltering angel so nothing can harm you. Laughter to cheer you. Faithful friends near you. And whenever you pray, Heaven to hear you."

It wasn't the words on the card that got me. It was the act of her giving it to me and telling me how much she loved me, and that she had meant to give it to me many years before, but felt it was important to give it to me then. We cried together, and we prayed for God to heal her. I'll remember that moment forever. Although we talked several times on the phone after I went back to Austin, that trip was the last time I spoke to my mom face to face – the last time I got to hug her. She slipped into a coma a week later, and God took her home to Heaven.

When I came to the hospital that last time, I still believed my mom would get better. I stood by her bedside and prayed for God to heal her. The doctor and nurses told me she probably wasn't going to wake up, and I was still in denial. After she took her last breath, I was in complete shock for days. My only comfort came from knowing she was in Heaven and no longer suffering. My mom received her complete healing, and I'm extremely grateful I was able to be by her side when she took her last breath. It was a tragedy I wasn't prepared for, and I was left feeling this huge void that no one could replace. Winter again chilled my soul.

I turned to God in my brokenness, and things seemed dark and bleak for a while. I got through it day by day with the help of God and my family. I focused on helping my stepdad get through it. He had given up on living; he begged for God to take him so he could be with her.

My mom was the rock in our family, and our whole landscape changed when she was gone. Everything was different and we had to adjust to a new normal. It was difficult, but we maneuvered through it with many tears and laughs in remembrance of a strong, beautiful woman. My stepdad passed away two years later, and I know he was extremely happy to finally be in Heaven with her.

I'm so thankful for that time of healing and remembering the good times with my mom. It was a tough season, but I came out stronger in many ways. During that time, I grew even closer to God. He was there for me every single time I needed Him.

The good news is that just like winter, tragedy is only for a season. It will end, and a new season will come. Many seeds were planted during that winter season, struggling just beneath the surface to peek out and grow. They were seeds of hope and faith, seeds of a new beginning – a new thing. I wanted my mom and stepdad to be proud of who they had helped me become – a strong woman of faith. I wanted to take my trials and tribulations that I had experienced over the years and turn them into something positive that would help others. God was at work beneath the surface, always guiding and directing me. It was time to fulfill my calling, and I was up for the challenge. God placed a vision in my heart, and I knew I needed to fulfill what He asked me to do.

When going through trials, tragedies, or tribulations, the pain and suffering are very real, and most of the time, life changing. In my life, when coming out of trials, I've used it as a catalyst for positive change. I've found beauty, peace, and joy in turning something bad or negative into something good or positive. It's easier to move forward teaching and helping others than it is to stay in misery, trying to find someone or something to blame. I choose every day to be strong and not give in to my insecurities. I have a purpose, and I don't want to live in fear anymore. In Romans 8:31, it says, *"If God is for us, who can be against us?"* God is my protector, my shield, and I trust that He will continue to be there for me through all of life's ups and downs.

There is beauty that comes from trials and tribulations. It's difficult to see it in the beginning, but it's there – waiting for the perfect opportunity to bloom. Once the landscape has been completely decimated, and the healing process has begun, it's time to plant seeds again. There is beauty in the changes that happen within yourself, and there is beauty when the landscape around you starts to grow again. It will look different but feel familiar, because it's still you.

Resting in God's Arms

In Jeremiah 29:11, the Lord declares that He knows the plans He has for me, and those plans give me hope and a future. What an amazing God we serve! I can only imagine the joy it brings Him to know that I'm ready for what He has planned for me.

After dwelling in the comfort of His arms, my faith is stronger, and my heart is aligned with His. So, as I walk out into the sunlight, ready to plant seeds and help others that are struggling in their faith, I take a deep breath and count my blessings, for they are many. My faith is in the One who created the earth and everything on it. A winter season makes me feel like I'm out in the wilderness, alone and desperate – but God is there with me. He protects and comforts me, and I'm forever grateful for His love. God will do the same for you.

In the Old Testament, Abraham also experienced a winter wilderness season, and God was there for him, too.

The Story of Abraham

Abraham is known as the "Father of Faith." He lived a comfortable life in the city of Ur. It was a prosperous city, but it was also where they performed pagan sacrifices. In Genesis 12:1, God directed Abraham to leave Ur. He was instructed to live in tents, and he obeyed God, even though he didn't know what God's plans were. Imagine living in a really nice home where you have everything you need. Family and friends are close by, and life is good. Then one day, God asks you to leave all of it behind and doesn't tell you where you're going, and you'll have to live in a tent for the entirety of the journey. Abraham had to have faith to set out on an unknown journey.

This was a spiritual winter season for Abraham. He walked and talked with God, and I'm sure their intimacy grew to great heights during Abraham's journey to the promised land. God also promised Abraham that he would be a father to many nations, and his offspring would be as many as the stars in the sky. Abraham believed God, and when he was one hundred years old, God fulfilled His promise, and Isaac was born.

Abraham's test of faith didn't end when Isaac was born. When Isaac was a teenager, God asked Abraham to take his son up to the mountain and offer him as a burnt offering. If I were Abraham, I would've questioned God. "But God, you said my offspring would be as numerous as the stars in the sky. If I do this, how will that happen?" But Abraham didn't question Him. He simply took his son and some wood for the offering and hiked up the mountain. I can't even imagine the thoughts that had to be going through Abraham's head. My heart would've been breaking, but Abraham trusted God with something as precious as his son.

When they got to the place God had designated for the sacrifice, he bound his son's hands and feet, and just as he was about to take his son's life with a knife, God stopped him and told him to sacrifice the ram that was in a thicket nearby. The faith of Abraham was monumental during this moment. He had to believe that God would either stop him from killing his son, He would resurrect him from death, or He would provide another son for him through his wife, Sarah. That is an amazing testimony of faith. He believed in the divine power of God Almighty. In Romans 4:20-21, it says that Abraham didn't waver, and was strengthened in his faith because he was fully convinced that God would do what He promised.

It was through his winter season with God that Abraham was able to build the kind of faith that it took to trust God with his only son. Through Abraham, seeds of faith were planted for many generations throughout history, and our faith today still stands on that same foundation.

The gift of life begins in the seed. I've learned that winter seasons are important for healthy growth in life. Restoration of the soul is God's specialty, and winter is that season. It's when I rest that God can shift my heart and mind to the deep things and help me focus on what will bring me true peace and joy. If God knows the number of hairs on my head (Luke 12:7), then He knows exactly what is taking place in every single seed that is planted in the ground. He knows whether it will grow into a mighty tree and how much fruit it will bear. God knows what He has planned for you in every season of your life. That includes the coronavirus pandemic we are currently experiencing. Yes, even now, God has a plan for you and your family. Rest in Him during those winter seasons and be prepared for that new beginning when spring finally comes.

CHAPTER TWO

CHAPTER TWO: SEED

Describe your favorite season. Why?

What is something that has happened during your winter season?

Have you ever had a salvation experience? Would you like to?

CHAPTER 3

Growth produces signs. After a long, cold winter season, the landscape no longer looks vibrant. As the earth thaws, it is often not pretty. But as spring arrives, the sun shines longer in the sky, and it's warmer outside. The land may be barren, but it's ready for seeds to rebirth. It's time to put the winter coat, sweaters, and long socks up, because spring is on its way.

When coming out of a spiritual winter season, I get excited for things to come. Tiny seeds of hope are all around me, and I'm ready to take what God taught me during my winter season out into the world.

Once a seed is planted in the ground and watered, germination begins to occur. Each seed has an embryo, and once the water reaches the embryo, the seed pod bursts, and the seed begins to sprout. A tiny radicle breaks free and begins to take root beneath the surface. This radicle becomes the primary root of the tree and secures it into the ground. With the right amount of water, oxygen, and sunlight, a sprout begins to form and comes out of the ground.

After being underground in the dark, it breaks through and upward into the light. The emerging sprout will continue to grow, eventually forming the beginning of a stem. There is no doubt that spring has arrived, and the landscape is ready for the changes that are coming. There are so many details that go into planting something as small as a seed, and you can be assured that God hasn't left any detail out of the changing seasons in the natural or spiritual realm.

If you've been through a winter season, and you're seeing that it's finally coming to an end, it's time for the next season. A new beginning is just what is needed to move forward. The seed of faith that was planted however long ago is ready to burst and take root deep in the center of your heart. God is waiting to show you all the beautiful things He has in store just for you. That seed of faith that was planted long ago is ready to make its debut. It will begin to grow, and hope will spring forth. It may start out small, but each day there is a change, and tiny blessings will grow into beauty all around you.

I remember the beginning of my faith walk. I was very excited and ready for this new thing. I wanted to be teachable, humble, and ready for whatever God had for me and my family. Hope began to spring forth, and I had a strong desire to move forward away from the old season and leaping with joy into the new season. At the time, I had no idea where my faith journey would take me, but I trusted God to show me the way. Besides attending church and going to Bible studies, I dove deep into God's word to learn more about all that He is. I discovered that everything I needed to know about life is in His Word. If I'm struggling in a specific area, I'll look up scriptures that apply to my circumstances, and after I read it, my situation gets less complicated and faith takes over.

The seed has sprouted, and change is on the horizon.

Seeds of Faith

During my most recent winter season, God showed me that the unity of His children is needed now more than ever before. That seed of faith was planted many years ago in another spiritual winter season, and I've been watering and nurturing it since then. His timing is always perfect, and now is the perfect time to grow that seed into a mature tree so it can produce fruit.

We are living in a time when America is becoming more and more divided. It's truly heartbreaking to see the changes that are taking place all around me. All I need to do is go to His word to get encouraged. Hebrews chapter 13:8 says, *"Jesus Christ is the same yesterday and today and forever."* The world has changed, but He hasn't. We must stand on faith together in unity and defeat the enemy of this world.

If God has planted a seed of faith in your heart during a spiritual winter season, He will provide all the tools needed for that seed to grow into a mighty tree. Trust in the process; have faith in God – He will guide you through it. When God first gave me the vision of *Standing on Faith Together,* I was in my mid-twenties. I'd just barely started going to church, and it was before I accepted Jesus. It was a tiny seed, and I had no clue of the depth of its meaning back then. It wasn't until my late thirties that He gave me a vision to write a book. I was so excited and ready to serve. The seed had finally sprouted. I thought He would take care of the vision He gave me at that time immediately, but His timeline isn't the same as mine. It needed time to be watered; it needed time to grow and mature. I believe and have insurmountable faith that He already knew the pandemic would happen in the year 2020. He knew what was going to happen in and around our world. He knew the perfect time to plant that winter seed many years ago, and He absolutely knew when it would grow into a mature tree that would produce amazing fruit. The message He gave me over twenty years ago has been growing and maturing *"for such a time as this."* (Esther 4:14) God deserves all the glory, for He knows all things.

God planted that seed of faith in my heart, and it was my job to grow it. When it finally sprouted, it was right before the economic crisis of 2008; a year before my world got turned upside down. It was hard work to keep that sprout alive. God wanted me to write about faith during a time that the only way I could have survived was to have complete faith in Him. I was angry and frustrated, but I persevered and learned so much about God during this season. My outlook on life completely changed, and I learned how to be grateful for the simple things in life.

If what God planted in your heart has sprouted, hold onto it. His perfect timing will be revealed to you at just the right time. Keep praying and seeking His wisdom. He'll show you the way.

New Beginnings

The season of spring represents new beginnings. It is refreshing after a cold winter season. Flowers bloom, birds sing, and animals awaken. When something new is birthed in my spirit, hope springs forth. Joy is my newfound friend, and my future suddenly becomes brighter. In a spring season, what used to look impossible changes to anything being possible. Amen! The change from winter to spring is complete, and I'm ready to go outside and bask in the sunlight.

The birth of something new is fragile, and it must be taken care of properly for it to grow. When a seed sprouts, it's still weak and in danger of disease or animal grazing. The same applies to my faith that has sprouted a new thing. The enemy wants to destroy it before it grows into a mature tree, because he doesn't want me to produce fruit for God's kingdom. During this fragile state, it's important for me to remember where my heart is rooted, which is in Jesus Christ. The more I depend on Him, the stronger I become. As I learn more about God, changes take place deep in my heart. The winter season becomes more distant, and I'm able to focus on the new things that are growing. As my heart is letting go of things that I've been holding onto, God is placing new things there. Bitterness is replaced with contentment, depression is replaced with joy, anxiety is replaced with peace, and pain is replaced with serenity.

God wants to restore all that is lost, and my faith is an assurance that full restoration will happen. Psalm 23:3 says:

"He restores my soul. He leads me in paths of righteousness for his name's sake."

It isn't a question of will He restore it, it's a matter of when He will restore it. When I was neck deep in debt after the recession, I couldn't see a way out of it. I felt like I was drowning, and I was exhausted from trying to keep my head above water. When I felt like giving up, I know God held me in His arms – encouraging me to hold on a little longer. He had a plan to restore all that I was going to lose, but I couldn't see it through my pain and frustration. As time went by, I began asking God to help me and my husband rebuild what we'd lost. God has done so much for us since coming out of that time when our lives were completely decimated. He's helped us rebuild what we lost, and we're faithfully working towards our financial goals at a steady pace. God is on my side, and I will no longer be afraid (Psalm 118:6).

As someone who has experience of great loss and extremely lean times, I understand the pain of that loss and the struggle of trying to move on from it. There are people that have experienced a great loss through fire, tornado, hurricane, tsunami, the death of a loved one, the coronavirus pandemic, or some other devastating tragedy. No matter what the tragedy is, it's difficult to move forward. I can also say from experience that it is possible. For me, I moved forward the only way I knew how – by having faith in God. He has healed the pain of that loss, and I am now using what I went through to help others.

In the Old Testament, the book of Nehemiah is a great example of someone that experienced decimation, and when Nehemiah asked God for help, He answered.

Standing on Faith Together – The Story of Nehemiah

King Artaxerxes was the king of Persia, and Nehemiah was a high official in the king's court. Nehemiah knew about the destruction of his home city, Jerusalem, and he was heartbroken. He wanted to rebuild it, and he prayed for God's help. Nehemiah brought the matter to King Artaxerxes and gained permission to rebuild Jerusalem.

In 445 B.C., the King appointed Nehemiah as the provincial governor of Judah. Nehemiah inspired others to join the cause, and they rebuilt the wall surrounding Jerusalem. These people stood on faith together in unity, and God provided every single thing they needed to rebuild Jerusalem. Nehemiah helped the poor rebuild their homes. He heard the cries of the people in his province and made sure all their outstanding debts were forgiven and their land was returned to them.

During this time, the enemies of Jerusalem were still plotting to destroy the city, even while they were rebuilding it. Even though the people of Jerusalem knew this, it didn't stop them. Nehemiah and the people of Jerusalem prayed through it, and God protected them. Tragedy had struck, and after a season of mourning, it was time to rebuild and plant seeds again. The people prayed together, and there was peace and harmony as they worked together for the same purpose.

God Makes A Way When There Is No Way

We have seen the story of Nehemiah repeated throughout history. When tragedy strikes, people want to help. Christians join together for the purpose of praying and helping others in desperate need. We stand united in faith and expect God to show up and perform miracles that only He can. After Hurricane Katrina hit in 2005, the city of New Orleans, Louisiana was completely destroyed. Several surrounding states also suffered massive damage. People from all around the United States came to help in whatever way they could. Food, water, supplies, and so much more came pouring in as the process of rebuilding began. Lives were forever changed because tragedy had struck in a monumental way. Our God is the same God that brought everyone affected by Hurricane Katrina through a devastating loss. He will get us to the other side of this worldwide pandemic, too. God will not leave out one single detail. Trust in Him.

Although it's sometimes hard to find, there is beauty in tragedy. Rebuilding someone's life after they have lost everything could be the best thing that has ever happened to them. They may have suffered a great loss, but it could have been the catalyst that changed their life for the better. The wonders of God are a mystery, but He knows what our future holds, and He'll guide each of us as we make our way to the other side of tragedy. When all you see before you is darkness and uncertainty, it's the perfect opportunity for God to show you that He'll make a way when there seems to be none. He did it for Nehemiah, Moses, and many others in the Bible. He'll do it for you. He's done it for me, and as I continue my faith journey, I know He'll do it again.

It may seem as though you are surrounded by wilderness, but God can see through the brush and trees. All that is required of you is faith. When Pharaoh was pursuing Moses, the people of Israel were afraid when they looked back and saw Pharaoh's army and when they looked in front of them all they saw was the Red Sea. There was nowhere for them to go. How were they going to survive an imminent attack? Moses told them to not be afraid. He raised his staff, the Red Sea parted, and every Israelite made it safely across to the other side. God made a way where there was no way. Isaiah 43:16-19 says it best:

> *"This is what the Lord says – he who made a way through the sea, a path through the mighty waters, who drew out the chariots and horses, the army and reinforcements together, and they lay there, never to rise again, extinguished, snuffed out like a wick: 'Forget the former things; do not dwell on the past. See, I am doing a new thing! Now it springs up; do you not perceive it? I am making a way in the wilderness and streams in the wasteland.'"*

What a joyous moment! God protected them at a time they had to be terrified. If you are terrified because of the pandemic, guess what? He'll protect you, too – have faith.

My husband has been a contractor for over a decade now. When he first started installing cable, internet, and phone, he was making good money. As I stated earlier, we were doing great financially – until the housing market crashed. Since then, the work hasn't been as steady, and I've been praying for *years* for God to open another door for my husband. I mean, when I tell you I've prayed – I've begged, pleaded, and sobbed over this request. Who can relate? If you've prayed for something desperately, and God finally answered your prayer, you'd understand.

A couple of years ago, my husband didn't work for an entire month, and things were really slow the first few months of the next year. I thought, *this is it. We're back to what we went through ten years prior.* I decided in my heart that I was going to have faith that God was going to answer this prayer, no matter what I was seeing. After months of this, I was once again praying, and God spoke to me and said, "I'm doing a new thing for your husband." I believed Him and continued to praise Him for several months over this "new thing" He was going to do in my husband's life.

Not long after that, my husband came to me and said a couple of guys he used to work with called him and asked if he wanted to come work with them. They used to be in the cable business, too, and they were doing something different. God immediately reminded me of the "new thing" He was going to do. I didn't hesitate in supporting my husband in his new venture. My husband is now splicing fiber, and he loves what he does. When God spoke the words, "I'm going to do a new thing," I didn't think to look it up in the Bible. It wasn't until I was writing this book that I came across the scripture above, and it brought me back to that moment. He once again made a way when I didn't see a way. Thank You, Father for always taking care of Your children. I so love You.

God will make a way now just as He did over 2000 years ago. In 2017, Hurricane Harvey hit the Texas coast and destroyed tens of thousands of homes and businesses, but it didn't stop God's plans for any of the people that were affected by that storm. It may have changed the course they were on, but there was no mistaking the unity that was seen and heard during that difficult time. The pandemic of 2020 won't stop what He has planted within your heart. If God gave you a vision of something, nothing will stop it from happening. Keep praying and nurturing that sprout. God will make a way where there seems to be no way.

Unity is Powerful

During this new and fragile spring season, it's important to stay focused on God and faith. It's the single most important thing that is needed to get you through anything that comes your way. Remember, the enemy doesn't want you to be successful with what God is doing in your life, so he'll try to distract you to get you off God's path. He has powerful tools that he uses to sidetrack you, and it's essential that you remember what your purpose is.

When my husband and I were running our small business, it gave me the opportunity to stay home with our children. I decided to homeschool them until each of them graduated high school. It was a blessing for me to teach and spend precious time with them. I never thought I would be qualified to teach them, but as I prayed, God showed me the importance of what I was doing for them, and how it would affect them later as adults. I poured all my heart into teaching them to the best of my ability, and it wasn't just Math, Science, English, and Social Studies. I taught them how to laugh and play together; to enjoy the good times, and how to smile through the bad times. I taught them how to pray to God, and I told them what Jesus did for each of them. I equipped them with everything I knew would help them become the best at whatever God has called each of them to do. It was one of the best times of my life.

There were many distractions and ploys the enemy tried to use during those valuable years, but I stayed focused on God. He qualified me to do what He called me for. It was my faith in Him during the difficult days (and there were many) that got me through it. There are many parents that have just experienced the joys of homeschooling due to the coronavirus pandemic. It's not an easy task. My respect for teachers went up tremendously when I started teaching my own children.

Faith and God's word are the keys to defeating the enemy and all his ploys to stop you. When you feel distracted or frustrated, remember the power of standing on faith together. Call your friends or family and ask them to pray with you – unity is powerful against the enemy. You have something that someone needs, and only you are qualified for it because God qualifies the called.

Whatever difficult task you are facing is not too hard for God. He knows, He sees, and He hears your prayers. Have faith and stay the course. Continue to learn and grow, preparing yourself for the next season. God's already there… waiting.

CHAPTER 3: SPROUT

What is your favorite thing about springtime? Be specific.

Have you ever participated in a group bible study? Why or why not?

What is something you have prayed about for a really long time?

CHAPTER 4

Summer is a spurt. Summer is also my favorite time of the year. Things are moving and shaking; there is activity all around me, and the sun is shining bright in the sky encouraging trees to grow to their great heights. The winter season is a distant memory that the warm sun chased away. It's time to work hard, but also a time to place my feet in the sand and gaze out over the ocean – taking in all the beauty that God created. It's time for diligently doing what God has called me to do, and it's also time for picnics and evening sunsets. Through my faith, God has shown me the beauty of what's in my heart – and when I'm doing what's in my heart, even though it's hard work, it brings me so much joy. I'm growing my faith while doing what I love. A tiny seed planted long ago grows quickly during the summer season.

In the warmth of summer, a seed sprout transitions to a sapling once it has grown to the height of three feet. As a sapling grows, branches begin to form on the small trunk, and roots begin to spread underground, making the tree even stronger. At this stage, a sapling is not yet able to bear fruit or reproduce seeds. This stage is similar to a child rapidly growing into a tall teenager. Saplings grow quickly, as do children. They consume every resource for growth put before them and gobble up food like they will never be full. Well on their way to maturity, they are preparing for all the fruit they will produce.

As the body of Christ, when we are growing in unity together, we experience wholeness or solidarity. In a summer season, we can be assured in faith that we are rapidly growing towards the assignment

God has placed in our heart. Summer is a time for development, and possibly even some growing pains. Bask in His light, maximize your faith, and learn all you can during this time with God.

Moses and His Monumental Faith

Like Noah, Moses was a great man of faith. He was chosen by God to be the leader of the Israelites. He went through all the stages of the tree – from a seed to a mature tree that produces good fruit – and God used him mightily. He learned and his faith grew abundantly. Moses was born as a Hebrew slave that should never have lived. Pharaoh was afraid that the slaves would try to take over Egypt, so he put out an order for all Hebrew baby boys to be killed at birth. Moses's mother decided to hide him in a basket and placed him by the side of the Nile River. Pharaoh's daughter came to the river to wash and found Moses nearby in his basket. She took him to the palace and raised him as her own son. Buried as a seed inside Pharaoh's palace, Moses knew he was a Hebrew and never forgot where he came from.

After watching an Egyptian beat a Hebrew slave to death, Moses killed him and fled to another country. It was during his time away that he grew like a sapling into the vessel he was created to be. God spoke to him and told him he needed to go back to Egypt and free the Hebrews from slavery. Moses questioned God because He didn't think he was the man for the job. He had a speech impediment that made him feel like he wouldn't be a good leader – God still wanted him. Moses had sinned – he had murdered someone, but God still called him to lead His people. God had fruit for him to bear.

I can relate to Moses in this. When God asks me to do something that I don't think I'm qualified for, I question Him. "God, are you sure you want *me* to do this? I really don't think I'm capable of doing what You're asking me to do."

No one looks forward to being stretched in growth. We love the summer season because of the sun! But it's the Son that speaks to me in the rapidly forced season of growth. He has lovingly reassured me every time that He is confident that I'll carry out the task He has set before me. Remember – God qualifies the ones He calls. He'll provide everything we need to carry out His purpose. I look back at the woman I was ten to twenty years ago and I want to hug her and whisper in her ear, "You got this! Roll with the summer."

Has God placed something in your heart that you think you can't do? When He asked me to write a book many years ago, I laughed, thinking "There is no way I'm capable of doing this, Lord. Are you sure this is what You want me to do?" And here we are, years later, and I'm writing just as He asked. What is that thing that keeps plaguing you? That one thought that won't leave your heart and mind? Start praying about it – God has a purpose for placing it within you. He will provide all you need to make that dream and vision come true.

Moses walked and he talked with God. His personal experiences with God are glorious, and it required insurmountable faith for Moses to carry out the task He chose him for. He provided everything Moses needed, just as He supplies us with everything we need for our assignments. God will continue to do this for each of us – all it takes is your faith.

Uncomfortably Going Deeper in Faith

Like with trees taking root deep in the ground, my faith is growing exponentially. The landscape that was barren previously is now alive and growing. It looks and feels different than it did before. I've learned to lean deeper into my faith when trials and tribulations come my way. I see things differently now than I did when I first started my faith walk. God has shown me the power of faith and unity, and I want to share the importance of this meaningful nugget that has taken root deep in my heart.

As I mentioned previously, my husband is a self-employed contractor. He's good at what he does, but he doesn't have a guaranteed income every week, and when he gets paid, it's never the same amount. Sometimes there are weeks that go by without a paycheck. It's hard to plan a budget around this type of income. I would love to tell you that it's something you get used to, but it's simply not true. It requires deep, abiding faith. We've learned to make smarter decisions with our money. It's been a roller-coaster ride for the past decade, but we made it through one of the most difficult times of our marriage – and we came out stronger. I can tell you with certainty that we wouldn't have survived without faith. To put it simply – it was tough.

During that time, there were too many things that were thrown at us, and some days were just more than I could handle. I spent a lot of time praying for God to help us. I shed many tears of frustration, hurt, and anger. I wanted to give up multiple times, and it was during those talks with God that He asked me to go deeper in my faith. It was time to trust the sun in the summer. The sun burns off all but the healthiest plants. It gives every healthy plant the photosynthesis it needs to feed itself.

So what does that mean for me? Going deeper in my faith meant I had to stop trying to figure everything out on my own. I considered myself a master at figuring things out, but I learned there were some things that I couldn't do without God. It meant reading the Bible more so I could learn from the people that have traveled similar paths before me. Sometimes it meant I just needed to sit and talk with God. One of the most important lessons I learned during that time was how much God loves it when I sit and talk with Him. It was the definition of me going deeper into my faith, and it helped me so much. I had to let some things be burned off and reach for Jesus to nurture my growth.

When I go deeper in my faith, I picture a huge tree, and I see myself nestled within the trunk of the tree. Jesus envelops me, allowing me to rest and draw strength from the only One that can help me during difficult times. I let go of what I see and trust that God will carry me and my family out of the darkness or tribulation. And guess what? He has, every single time. He brought my husband and me out of a difficult season with many lessons learned. He changed the direction of the path we were on, one that didn't have curvy, treacherous, or bumpy roads, or hills that drop off suddenly. It's a simple, straight, clear, and smooth path.

As I went deeper in my faith during that searing hot summer season, I discovered a precious time that helped build my faith. As I'm growing, I'm learning, and my faith is strengthened. The bond that I have with God is unbreakable. I still have questions. I don't have all the answers I need to be successful at what He's called me to do. To find those answers, I need to continue to go deeper in my faith, so I don't make mistakes or get distracted. I pray for the Holy Spirit to guide me and keep me on His path. As I'm walking this path, the landscape continues to grow, and true change is happening all around me.

True Change is Happening

How do you measure true change? True change for me is when I noticed the changes taking place in the way I thought or how I responded to things. My heart is filled with love for God's people, and when I was living selfishly, it was something I never even considered. True change is when I began to focus less and less on the things of this world, and more on the things of God. I chose to look at people with the love of Jesus instead of hate, because hate never gets us anywhere good. Jesus said to love your neighbor as you love yourself (Matt. 22:39). He didn't say love them only if they deserve it or love them as long as they don't make you mad. He said love them, and that's what I chose to do. A change took place in my heart because of my faith. God shows each of us His heart of love when we pursue a relationship with Him.

I remember when I used to be selfishly focused on what I wanted, and I'm thankful I no longer live that way. It was evidence of the summer growth with God. In my immaturity, I had a strong desire to be first, and I didn't care whose feelings I hurt along the way.

I'll tell you a story that God reminds me of occasionally, and it's humbling for me to talk about it. My oldest son joined the Marine Corp., and he had just completed boot camp in Camp Pendleton, CA. They have a ceremony for graduating Marines, and my family and I flew to California to watch and celebrate with my son. I had no idea there would be so many people there, and I wanted to be at the front so I could get a good look at my son as he walked by. My husband and family weren't as insistent as I was to get closer, but I was determined. I slowly kept inching my way up closer to the front, and as I did this, I could tell that some people were getting agitated, but I didn't care – I was getting to the front no matter what. I was about three-fourths of the way up there when I heard a woman make a nasty remark that didn't sit well with me.

Just to give you a better understanding of the atmosphere – it was extremely quiet. No one was talking because if we did, you couldn't hear what the speaker was saying. The woman's comment irritated me, so I popped off with my own nasty comment, (I don't remember exactly what I said, but I know it wasn't kind) and a loud argument ensued. *Everyone* was looking at the two of us, and I could see my family towards the back, staring at me with looks of disbelief on their faces. The woman not-so-kindly explained that she got there early, and I should have done the same if I wanted to be at the front. I knew I was in the wrong, but I was committed to my stubbornness, and basically told her to shut up and get over herself. I stood my ground and stayed in that spot through the entire process, and I didn't enjoy it one bit because I was so mad at that woman for embarrassing me. Oh, how wrong I was. This happened several years after I accepted Jesus – which makes it even more humiliating.

I should have never been mad at the woman for stating the obvious, and she didn't embarrass me – I embarrassed myself and my family. God has used that scenario several times to remind me of who I used to be. True change happened within my heart as I continued to learn more about God. I can see it now, but I didn't have a clue before I had a relationship with God.

Have No Fear

The chains that kept me bound in my past are no longer holding me down. Since the day of my salvation, I no longer fear the enemy of my soul. I remember when my youngest daughter was eight or nine years old, and she suddenly became afraid of everything. She couldn't sleep by herself, and she wouldn't leave my side during the day. She loved going to kids' church, but during that time, she refused to go in without me. She told me that bad things were going to happen to her or me, and she needed to be with me. This went on for several weeks, and no matter how much I assured her that she didn't need to have this fear, it didn't do any good. She cried often, and when I asked her what was wrong, she said simply, "I'm scared, Mommy."

It broke my heart, and I knew I had to do something about it. I told one of the youth leaders at our church what had been happening, and after talking and praying about it, we knew it was something deeper. The youth leader looked up all the scriptures she could find in the Bible that related to fear. I began reading these scriptures every single day to my daughter until she had most of them memorized. Within a week, it was gone as suddenly as it came. She has never had an issue with the spirit of fear since. There is power in God's Word – and we are set free when we speak it. My daughter remembers it well, and she learned a valuable lesson that she will carry with her for the rest of her life. God didn't give us a spirit of fear; He gave us a spirit of power, love, and a sound mind (2 Tim. 1:7). As my heart changed, God has given me peace and strength in the areas I used to be afraid. All of it can be attributed to the tree of living water, the different seasons I've gone through, and my faith. Have no fear – God is with you always.

What do you fear? My current biggest fear is rejection – it's the main reason I'm terrified to write a book and put myself out in the world.

I'm praying through it every single day, and I know if God asked me to do something for Him, I shouldn't fear anything. Jesus was rejected, but He still made a significant impact here on earth. My hope and prayer is that through my obedience to God, I'll save someone from an eternity in Hell.

What's Next?

I spend more time in prayer with God than I ever have. Before, I always felt rushed, and sometimes skipped talking to Him at all. I have broken off bad habits that weren't good for me, and I'm thankful to God for changing my heart. The difference in my relationship with God since I've changed these habits has been astonishing and life changing. He listens when I want to laugh and be silly. He hears my voice when I cry out to Him, or when I'm contemplating life. He speaks to me in ways that only I understand. His love surrounds me, and I'm grateful for a God that loves me no matter how many mistakes I make. As I let go of the way I used to do things, peace enters my heart and mind, and God shows me how He meant for things to be.

By the time the summer season has ended, we are tired of the hot, sweaty days and longing for some cooler temperatures. The leaves begin to turn yellow, orange, red, and brown as they fall to the ground. The atmosphere changes to excitement for the busy harvest season ahead. Fall is here, and this scripture comes to mind:

> *"as it is written: 'What no eye has seen, what no ear has heard, and what no human mind has conceived' – the things God has prepared for those who love him"* (1 Cor. 2:9).

It's time to reap the harvest that has been sowed over the past few seasons. All the lessons I've learned and all my hard work will finally be rewarded, and I'll give God the glory for all that He has done for me and my family. He continues to prepare me for the next season – a season filled with joy and bounty – a season of harvest.

CHAPTER 4: SAPLING

What is the best summer you have ever experienced?

What is an area that you have grown rapidly in? How?

What area do you sense God is calling you to grow in?

CHAPTER 5

Autumn is fruitful. The fall season has arrived, and the tree has grown to its full maturity. It's time for the harvest. Finally! Fruit is bountiful, and the tree has many branches on the trunk. The roots of the tree are anchored deep into the ground. As a Christian, my faith is rooted deep in Jesus – my Savior – the One who has taught me about true love and saved me from an eternity in Hell. He didn't give up on me, and I won't give up on Him.

A fall season means it's time to reap the harvest of what has been sown. This time of the year is special because it's a season of giving and sharing. God has promised each of us a season of harvest. The blessing of these promises will be *"exceedingly abundantly above all that we ask or think"* (Eph. 3:20). Prepare for the blessings that are coming your way, because our God is good.

During this season of thanksgiving and blessings, God is rejoicing with each of us. He's proud of what we've accomplished, and He's cheering for us in Heaven. The fall season brings memories of pumpkin carving, hayrides, candy corn, and family gatherings. Laughter abounds and joy surrounds our homes and hearts. Our cup overflows with God's blessings. It was worth the wait.

A Mature Spiritual Tree

Getting to the mature fruiting stage takes time, courage, wisdom, faith, and a lot of fight. Let me put it to you this way – it ain't gonna be easy! Many times, the stillness of winter, the transformation of spring, and the rapid changes of summer bring us to the point of crying. Giving up would have been so much easier than continuing the fight, but as I mentioned earlier, it's through the fight that true transformation happens. The autumn season is filled with the fruit of the fight.

Psalm 126:5-6 says:

"Those who sow with tears will reap with songs of joy. Those who go out weeping, carrying seed to sow, will return with songs of joy, carrying sheaves with them."

There is one thing I'd like to say here: if you've reached this stage, I'm proud of you. You did it! The blessings that come from a harvest season are wonderful. You deserve everything that God has for you. Your journey may not have been beautiful, or you might not have a glorious story to tell, but none of that matters because you fought, and you didn't give up. So, let me say it again – *I'm proud of you!* And let me remind you that you're connected to the tree of living water; you're connected with Christ's followers all around the world. We are the hands and feet of Jesus, and we're called to serve our Lord. We're all standing with you, battered and bruised – but faithful to God Almighty. Just as He was with you during all the previous seasons of your life, He's with you in this season of harvest. Now it's time to sit back and enjoy the fruits of your labor. It's time to reflect on the many changes that have come in and out of your life. You made it. It's time for the seeds of faith that are coming from your mature spiritual tree to change other people's hearts towards the things of God.

Love Changes People

Love is a fruit. Love has a harvest. It grows in the intensity of summer, but can be recognized in the grace of autumn. I've witnessed many lives change through love.

I met a young man named Brad a few years ago, and he told me an amazing story that changed his life forever. While he was growing up, Brad never really knew his father, and his mother suffered from bipolar disorder and depression. She didn't work and most days she couldn't even get out of bed. They didn't have enough food to eat, and Brad told me he didn't have new clothes, or toys and games like most other kids his age. He also told me his home was never clean, and he never had his own room or bed. He knew his family was different than others, and as he grew older, he begged his mother to get help – she never did. The reality was, Brad's mother wasn't mentally healthy enough to provide for the needs of her child.

When Brad was about ten years old, he met someone his age at church, and they became fast friends. His friend's parents welcomed him into their home, and he loved everything about what they offered, because he'd never experienced that in his own home. He eventually moved in with them, and his friend's parents became his parents. They raised him like he was their own child; providing food, clothes, and his own room with a bed and furniture – a space he could call his own. Having these things brought him a lot of comfort, but what he was really experiencing was the fruit of their loving him.

While living with his friend, Brad struggled with feelings of hurt and anger. Leaving his mom affected him deeply, and even though he knew it upset her, he felt he made the right decision for himself because his life completely changed for the better when he moved in with his friend. As a child, he didn't know how to help her. As an adult, he now understands that she was suffering from a lifetime of depression, and as much as he wanted her to get help, she continued to refuse it. He's checked on his mother over the years, but said she still hasn't changed. There is nothing to harvest.

I recently spoke to Brad again, and he's grown into a mature young man that recently got married. I asked him how he was doing, and he told me he was doing really well, but he still sometimes struggled with the rejection of his mother's love. He felt like he wasn't good enough in some way, so that's why she never got better. The one question that always came to mind when he thought of his mom was: Why didn't his mother love him enough to change? He felt rejected and abandoned. The wounds still haven't completely healed, but now that he's older, he's learning how to mend the broken pieces of his heart.

Love. Brad's life was completely changed by the love of strangers. Why didn't this mother change for her son? The pain she suffered must be deeply rooted in her heart, so much so that it took over the love she should have had for her son. I've never met her, but I have empathy because she suffered so greatly. May the love of God reach to the very depths of her heart and heal the brokenness that tortures her. In Jesus's name. Amen.

Although things started out rough for Brad, he decided to move forward with his lovely wife, and spends a lot of time with his childhood friend and the parents that truly raised him. His friend's family changed the course of his life. Before he met them, he never understood simple things that most people take for granted – like moral values and the good feeling someone gets when they work hard and reap the benefits of their hard work. When he was a child, he missed a lot of school because his mother was too ill to understand the importance of Brad's education. Now he understands the value of learning, and he's currently in college working towards his bachelor's degree. He's grateful and thankful for the love of his friend's parents.

This story had a good ending. Brad's life completely *changed* because one family showed him the love, guidance, and discipline that every child needs to be a successful adult. Brad's story could have ended up very differently. What I left out of the story above was Brad had a sister that was a couple of years older than him. Her name is Samantha, and when Brad was young, Samantha began to show signs of bipolar disorder and depression like his mother. Samantha became a drug addict at a very young age, and she was cruel to Brad. There were some days he feared for his life. Samantha is still living at her mother's home and has several children of her own. Because she struggles with many of the same things their mother did, those children are being raised the same way Brad and Samantha were. It saddens me to tell you that Samantha's story did not turn out as positive as Brad's.

I believe God will use Brad's pain and testimony to help others someday. God rescued him, and his life completely changed. His future is bright, and I pray that Brad shares the love of God to many others and maybe his little nieces and nephews.

Have you or someone you know been changed by the love of God? 1 Peter 4:8 says:

"Above all, love each other deeply, because love covers over a multitude of sins."

Love changes people. And with the division we are experiencing in our world today, we need more love than ever before.

Changes are needed in our world today, the kind of changes that affect the deepest part of our hearts where all the hurt and rejection reside. The kind of changes that begin with a small seed of faith and transform into a mighty, mature tree. The kind of changes that reflect the love of God. The kind of changes we can accomplish through God.

The Love of God

The love of God covers all things, and nothing can separate us from His love. There isn't anything that isn't transformed or changed when the love of God touches it.

"For I am convinced that neither death nor life, neither angels nor demons, neither the present nor the future, nor any powers, neither height nor depth, not anything else in all creation, will be able to

separate us from the love of God that is in Christ Jesus our Lord."
(Rom. 8:38-39)

I was a teacher for a short time at a private school, and there was a young man that was always getting into trouble. His name was Jeremiah, and he was eleven years old. The only thing I knew about him was that his mother was a recovering drug addict, and he'd been in and out of foster homes most of his short life. He wasn't one of my students, but his class had recess at the same time my class did.

One day, Jeremiah was bullying another young boy on the playground. One of my students, Josh, walked over to Jeremiah and asked him to stop being mean to the boy he was picking on. Jeremiah got very close to Josh, and as they were staring at each other eye to eye, he spit in Josh's face. I was trying to make my way over to them quickly, because I was just sure Josh was going to punch Jeremiah in the face, but he didn't. Josh stepped back and wiped the spit from his face and told the boy that was getting bullied to go find his teacher. He then looked at Jeremiah and said, "I'm not sure what's going on in your life that has you so angry all the time, but I'm here if you want to talk." Jeremiah didn't know what to say and walked away.

A few weeks later, I was in the gymnasium with a couple of students from my class – Josh was one of them. We were working on a project for the principal. We heard shouting outside the gymnasium, and just as I was about to go see what was happening, Jeremiah busted the gymnasium door open with his teacher right behind him. Her patience had come to an end with this troubled young man. She asked if I could stay with Jeremiah until she called his mother. I said yes. What took place next could have only been orchestrated by God.

Jeremiah sat in a chair, crying. I walked over to him and asked if I could speak to him; he shrugged his shoulders. I didn't ask him what had just happened because it didn't matter. I simply started speaking words of love over him. I told him he was loved; he said he wasn't. I told him that God loved him; he said God could never love someone like him. I then told him that the students that were standing nearby loved him. He still didn't believe me. The other students walked over to him, and Josh – the young man that Jeremiah spit on, placed his hands upon Jeremiah's shoulders and began to pray for him. We prayed the love of Jesus over him as he sobbed. He hugged me, Josh, and the other students, and told us no one had ever shown him unconditional love like that. It was a rich experience for all of us who were standing on faith together for this young man.

For the rest of that school year, I witnessed a change in Jeremiah. He started to come out of his shell and even made a few friends. Every time he saw me, he ran up and gave me a big hug. After that school year ended, Jeremiah moved, and I never saw him again. But I'm confident that the love of God touched him, and it changed him forever. God used Josh to show Jeremiah the love He had for him, and He used me and a few other students to seal the deal. We were His hands and feet.

His Hands and Feet

Now that the tree has grown to its full maturity, it's time to examine this full-grown tree. They provide much more than seeds and fruit. Trees provide shelter for insects, birds, and many other animals. They also provide oxygen for us to breathe. Trees need us just as much as we need them. While trees take in carbon dioxide and breathe out oxygen, humans breathe in oxygen and breathe out carbon dioxide. It's a perfect fit! The different parts of a tree are the roots, crown, leaves, branches, and the trunk. Each of them serves a very specific purpose.

The roots are the most important part of the tree. The tree is anchored into the ground with roots beneath the surface. These roots intertwine with roots from neighboring trees, and together they form a strong support system. The main purpose of roots is to collect water and nutrients from the soil providing what is needed to help the tree grow.

The crown of the tree consists of the branches and leaves that are at the top. This provides shade for protection against the sun. Leaves provide food for the tree through photosynthesis. This process converts energy from the sun into sugars and starches. Leaves also convert carbon dioxide into oxygen. Branches provide support for the leaves and fruit on the tree.

The final part of the tree is the trunk. It provides the shape of the tree, and is used to transport water and nutrients to the branches and leaves. It's a lot of work being a tree, and as you read above, they play a very important role here on earth.

As a Christian and a mature spiritual tree, I also have a very important role here on earth. My faith is anchored deep in Jesus, and my support system is God and the body of Christ. Jesus said in John 15:5 that He is the vine, and we are the branches. The vine is the trunk of the tree. I'm connected to Jesus through my spiritual tree. My role is to provide seeds for others to plant, and as their roots begin to grow, they will intertwine with the roots of other mature spiritual trees, and we will all become stronger in Christ together. As the crown of the tree grows, we (Jesus and I) are providing protection for others that are struggling or exhausted during their journey. We provide shelter, rest, and fruit for them to become strong again so they can continue their journey. I can't do this on my strength and will alone. Jesus is my strength, and only with Him can I be strong for others. John 15:4 clarifies this:

> *"Remain in me, as I also remain in you. No branch can bear fruit by itself; it must remain in the vine. Neither can you bear fruit unless you remain in me."*

We can't survive everything the devil throws at us without each other, without Jesus, or without God – our protector and champion.

In the second part of John 15:5, Jesus said we are the branches. Picture a mature tree in your mind. The tree is tall with many branches reaching up and out. There are many smaller branches coming from the larger branches. Remember, the trunk of the tree represents Jesus. These branches belong completely to the trunk of the tree. They get their food and nourishment from the trunk. For branches to survive, they must depend on the trunk for nourishment, strength, support, and vitality. As branches, we are the hands and feet of God.

It's my destiny here on earth to fulfill what God has called me to do, and knowing that I'm connected to the tree of living water with so many other Christians that are working to fulfill what God has called each of them to do is just beautiful to me. We are unified with Jesus, and there is power in that unity. It's time for us to allow God to reveal His power through the unified body of Christ.

Our world is struggling with spiritual blindness. Paul talks about this in 2 Corinthians, Chapter 4. He tells us that we, as Christians, have received God's mercy, and we don't handle God's word deceitfully. But to those that do not believe, the god of this age (devil) has blinded them so they cannot see God's light shining on them. There are a lot of people that are spiritually blind and deaf to the Holy Spirit's correction. They need to be awakened from their spiritual death so they can experience freedom in Christ just as we do. Friends, it's time for a revival. The coronavirus pandemic has brought so much of our country's brokenness to light, and it's time for us to unite and *stand on faith together* to promote change and the love of God. He has prepared each of us for this revival. Are you ready?

As I've said before, we're all connected to the tree of living water – God's tree. Our tree. As we *stand on faith together*, we're letting the enemy of our soul know he can't and won't win the battle for our souls. God already has the victory!

Pruning is Necessary

As the bountiful harvest season comes to an end, it's time to prepare for the winter season. This is the perfect opportunity to prune trees because they are dormant during winter. Removing branches during any other season could damage the tree permanently, and it may not recover. Pruning a tree is important for many reasons. It can influence the way a tree grows. If a tree is growing at an odd angle, pruning helps reshape it the correct way. Pruning also removes any dead branches, which allows room for new growth on the tree. It helps deter bug or animal infestation that could harm the tree. The right amount of pruning will ensure the tree produces bountiful fruit, and prolong the life of the tree.

Pruning is equally important on my spiritual tree. Jesus says in John 15:1-2:

> *"I am the true vine, and my Father is the gardener. He cuts off every branch in me that bears no fruit, while every branch that does bear fruit, he prunes so that it will be even more fruitful."*

God is the One who lovingly prunes anything in my life that is not producing good fruit. He knows what is holding me back, and as I'm praying for His help, He cuts the dead things out of my life. Sometimes, this can be painful, but it's for my benefit.

Have you ever wondered why someone you care about suddenly disappears from your life? It could be that God knows this person will not help you bear good fruit. He takes the things that aren't good for you away, so they won't cause further harm to you or your family. I've learned quite a few difficult lessons from God's pruning. At the time it was happening, it hurt, and I was frustrated. But when I look back on it now, I know it was God showing me He had something better for me. My faith is very important during this time of pruning, because I must trust God with every part of my life – especially my blind spots. If I don't see that something is holding me back or causing harm, I have faith that God sees it, and He'll remove it.

What has God pruned or cut away from your life? I have a list of things that He's pruned or cut away. One of them is raunchy romance novels. I've always loved to read, but as I was praying for God to show me anything in my life that was holding me back from my destiny, He showed me the romance novels. Reading is one of my favorite hobbies, and I was frustrated that God would ask me to stop doing something I enjoyed, but He had a purpose. Shortly after I stopped reading the naughty romance novels, He asked me to start writing for Him. God has a plan for your life – I encourage you to listen to what He's saying to you. It will change your life.

Dead branches on God's tree or the tree of living water represent people that say they are saved, yet they produce no fruit. How do you produce good fruit? The answer can be found in Galatians 5:22:

"But the fruit of the Spirit is love, joy, peace, forbearance, kindness, goodness, faithfulness, gentleness and self-control."

When we are *truly* connected to the tree of living water, we'll produce the fruits of the Spirit listed above. Only God knows the true status of our heart, and He is the one that decides whether or not someone must be cut away from His tree.

God not only cuts the dead branches away, but He also prunes the branches that are bearing fruit. Yes, even the good branches need to be pruned so they can produce more fruit. A mature tree produces sap, which consists mostly of water. Sap provides vital mineral nutrients to all parts of a tree. It's important to trim shoots or tiny stems from fruit-bearing branches, so that more sap can flow through the branches, which in turn provides more delicious fruit. God does the same thing for each of us. He prunes the fruit-bearing branches in our spiritual tree so we can produce more fruit.

My faith in God gives Him full access to my heart. It allows Him to shake my spiritual tree to let anything that doesn't belong fall away. I trust in His ability to remove obstacles that are keeping me from my destiny. I have faith that God will continue to prune and shape my spiritual tree so I can produce bountiful fruit that pleases Him. He will do the same for you.

Compassion for the Lost

As a mature Christian, my heart hurts for the people that don't know God. I want the lost to see and experience the love of God, and that can only come from the body of Christ. When Jesus was going from town to town, He spread the good news of the kingdom, and He healed diseases and cast out demons. He could have become tired, frustrated, or irritated, and at any point said, "This is too hard." But He didn't. In Matthew 9:36 it says:

"When he saw the crowds, he had compassion on them, because they were harassed and helpless, like sheep without a shepherd."

Instead of growing weary, He had compassion for the lost. Jesus could see the pain in people's hearts; He could see how they were tormented from their past. He knew they needed His help. That is pure love. He didn't judge or speak badly about them. He simply loved them.

To have that kind of love for people is what I strive for every day – even the people that cut me off while I'm driving or the ones that don't have the same views that I do. I don't know what's going on in their lives that would cause them to act this way, but I do know they need God's grace and love, just like I do.

Jesus promises us in Matthew 9:37 that we will have a plentiful harvest, but He also says, *"…the workers are few."* Harvest time reflects blessings, but it's hard work. This work takes patience and perseverance, and unfortunately these two things are lacking in many people. I know this is hard to hear, but Jesus spoke these words over two thousand years ago, and they are still true today. God is looking for hard workers that want to reap His blessings. He's calling each of us to do His work, and I want you and me to be counted among His hard workers.

My heart grieves for those that are struggling in their faith. If I could just sit down with them and explain that it's going to be okay, and they *will* make it through the pain of their tribulation with faith and the love of God, then my job is done. What area are you struggling in your faith? Please share at the end of this chapter. And know that if you are reading this, you are covered in prayer and strength.

His Beautiful Love

Jesus doesn't look at us with natural eyes, He sees us with spiritual eyes. So many people said and did hurtful things to Him, yet nowhere in the Bible does it say that Jesus cursed or tried to harm the ones that were doing these things. It's difficult to do that if you've been hurt by someone, or if someone you love has been hurt. Even as a mature Christian, I still find it difficult to have compassion for those I feel don't deserve it. It's just one more reason why my faith is so important. I trust that as I pray for those that have hurt me or have hurt someone I love, God will take care of it. I don't know what He knows about this person, but I know He's a just God. I pray they ask for forgiveness and change their ways to reflect the love of God, and I pray that they are transformed by His love, just like so many others.

When I do get upset, God gently reminds me that I'm not perfect either. I've said and done some things that I'm not proud of, and God loves me anyway – so I choose to have compassion on the lost just as God has compassion for me. They need God's love to guide them into His arms, and my hope is, *together*, we will reflect God's love to the many that are lost. Our faith in God will take care of the rest. His love never fails. We can be successful at many different things, but if we don't have love, then we have nothing (1 Cor. 13:1-3).

I remember many years ago, I prayed and asked God to show me the love He has for His children, and He gave me a glimpse of it. I was at work in downtown Dallas, and I was sitting at my desk. His love fell on me like a heavy blanket, and it brought me to my knees. It was overwhelmingly beautiful, and it literally took my breath away. For a few moments, I couldn't breathe. There was so much peace, joy, and a love so *felt* it was almost as if I could reach out and touch it. I wept, because it was glorious. I never want to forget those few short moments that God allowed me to experience the love He has for *all* things He created. What an amazing God we serve!

Standing Together

As the harvest season comes to an end, I ask that you remember all the blessings that God has showered on you. Reflect on the lessons you've learned and teach others what He's taught you. As a mature spiritual tree, you're ready to unite with fellow Christians all around the world. You're ready to stand with them, and you're prepared for any battle that comes your way. Together, we'll use all the tools God has provided for us to defeat the enemy of our souls. It won't be easy, but God already has the victory. We'll look to Him for guidance and direction, and in Him our faith abides forever and ever. Amen.

CHAPTER 5: MATURE TREE

Do you decorate for autumn? How?

How has someone blessed you with the fruit of their life?

Are you in a season of fruitfulness or are you being pruned? Explain.

CHAPTER 6

The pandemic of 2020 changed the entire world. As I'm writing this book, we are still knee deep in this crazy coronavirus pandemic. Our landscape looks different now. Gone are the days of hopping into your car and going to the lake or going to watch a movie. Now it's mandatory to reserve a spot prior to attending because they can only allow so many individuals in a confined space. When social distancing, at least six feet of space is required between you and another person. I'm going to be honest – it's weird and frustrating. Some countries are experiencing it worse than others, while in the United States, some states are experiencing it worse than others. It makes it difficult to travel. Actually, it's difficult to do anything right now.

Many businesses have closed their doors forever, because everything was shut down for a couple of months and they could not sustain the costs without income. As the government allowed things to slowly open back up, these businesses were not making enough money to survive, and there are many more that are barely hanging on. This means a lot of people are without jobs and are struggling to survive. We don't know what the long-term effect is going to be to our economy, but the longer this goes on, the deeper we fall into an economic crisis.

While some have a strong fear of this virus, others think it's ridiculous because we've encountered viruses before and have survived. For me, it's simple – my faith is in God, not man. I have chosen to focus on Him and the good things that have come out of this. There are many stories that have surfaced during this crazy time that show that people *want* to help other people. For example, healthcare workers that are exposed to coronavirus every day are scared to go home because they don't want to bring the virus to their spouse or children. Doctors and nurses are sleeping at hotels to keep their families safe, and they're not sure when they will be able to go home.

Emily Phillips is the wife of a doctor, and they have three children. She was concerned for their children, so she reached out on Facebook asking if anyone had an RV they could borrow to park outside of their home so her husband could come home each night and still see his family, even if from a distance. Holly Haggard responded and told Emily she could borrow her RV for as long as it was needed. Emily was immediately relieved of a lot of stress, and after seeing the need was so great, she and Holly created RVs 4 MDs. People from all over the United States were offering up their RV for free to any healthcare worker that was in need. What a blessing for people to come together and help others they don't even know. To find out more, go to their Facebook page: facebook.com/RVs4MDs.[1]

There was another story on goodnewsnetwork.org of an anonymous woman in Maryland that was making hundreds of bagged lunches and placing them on a table at a busy intersection. Many people had lost their jobs, and money was tight, so this woman wanted to help. She hung a sign by the table letting people know she would continue to do it as long as it was needed.[2] This kind gesture has helped many people that were concerned about what they were going to eat.

Although this pandemic has changed our way of life, it's amazing to see the good that is still out there in this very divided world. Fear of this virus is all over the news and social media. It's difficult to know when this virus will finally come to an end, because just as we think things are getting better, the media posts that things are getting worse. If I didn't have faith, I would easily get caught up in the fear and chaos that is being portrayed all around me. I know my God already knew about this, and I trust that He has a purpose for all that is going on.

A New Normal

What should we expect after this pandemic ends? A new normal is taking over right in front of us. Most states are requiring individuals to wear masks in public. No one can go into any building without wearing it per the new government regulations. The Center for Disease Control (CDC) have been working on a vaccine for the coronavirus for several months, and some government officials are pushing that it be mandatory for every person to get this vaccine when it becomes available. It's crazy to think how quickly we all submitted to what the government has asked us to do. As a Christian, I see and hear all that is going on, and I take all of it with me when I go to God in prayer. Every time I pray about this pandemic, God's answer is the same: "Don't focus on the pandemic, focus on what I've asked you to do." He's asked me to write this book and get His message out to His children. That has helped me more than any news I've watched or anything I've read on social media. There is work to be done for the kingdom of God, and that is where I'll continue to place my focus.

What is God calling you to do? When this pandemic first hit and we were forced to stay at home, it gave each of us precious time to ourselves. The busy nature of life slowed down for a short time and allowed God to speak to those places in our hearts and minds that only He can reach. For me, I've known for a while that God wanted me to write for Him, but my busy life got in the way. God spoke to me during the quiet days we were shut down, and He said, "It's time." Before this pandemic, I tried figuring out exactly how I was supposed to be a successful writer when I knew nothing about the business. But when God said it was time, everything began to line up.

I began praying for God to align me with someone to help me accomplish what He asked me to do. A couple of weeks went by, and one day I saw a post from a woman that intrigued me. She was a developmental editor, illustrator, and the author of three number one best-selling books on Amazon.com. I sent her a message; we set up our first meeting, and things took off from there. She has helped me in more ways than just writing. She has helped me shift my focus to things that I never even thought of before I met her. She's helped me find my voice for God, and she's helped me find the courage and confidence to be who God has called me to be. I'm grateful for her wisdom and guidance. I highly encourage you to find a mentor/coach too!

When we were shut down for a couple of months, I was able to take some much-needed time to think about what I've accomplished in my life – and I realized I'm not done. I have more life to live and many more assignments to complete. At the end of this chapter, I would like you to write down what you felt God was saying to you during those quiet months. What is it going to take for you to accomplish what He showed you? I can tell you with certainty that you'll need faith – even if it's as small as a mustard seed.

I'm not sure exactly what God is going to do with the book I'm currently writing, or the others I feel in my spirit He wants me to write, but I do know this: I have faith that it will reach the people He wants it to, and my prayer is that their life will forever be changed for the glory of God. Have faith and trust in Him, I promise you that He'll take care of the smallest details.

If you're not exactly sure what God is calling you to do, seek Him and faithfully pray for His guidance and direction. He won't fail you, and as I mentioned before, He's looking for diligent, hard workers. That means that there are plenty of opportunities for you in your future. When it's time for what God has called you to do, He'll make a way when it seems that every door is closed. When it's time, God will show up and things will fall into place. An example of His perfect timing is displayed masterfully in the book of Esther.

Esther Was Just A Girl

The book of Esther has ten chapters and is written beautifully. It's full of suspense, beautiful women, and a magnificent plot twist.

Esther was a young, beautiful Jewish woman. She was just a girl that was chosen among hundreds of other women by King Xerxes to be his queen. She was raised by her cousin Mordecai because her parents died when she was young. She found favor with many people in the palace, and King Xerxes was head over heels in love with her.

Now Esther never told the king or anyone at the palace that she was Jewish, because Mordecai instructed her not to. He feared for her life. King Xerxes appointed a loyal officer over all the nobles in his kingdom. His name was Haman, and he hated the Jewish people. When anyone came into Haman's presence, they were expected to kneel at his feet. Mordecai refused to kneel, and this angered Haman, so he began plotting how he was going to kill Mordecai and all the Jews. This information made its way to Esther, and she was distraught. Mordecai asked her to go to King Xerxes and beg for his mercy.

This wouldn't be an easy task. The king had to summon her; she couldn't just walk up to him and ask if she could talk to him. And if any man or woman approached the king in the inner court without being summoned, the king's law stated they were to be put to death unless he extended his gold scepter to them. Ah, but here is the beautiful part of this story. Esther relayed all this information to Mordecai, and his response was:

> *"If you remain silent at this time, relief and deliverance for the Jews will arise from another place, but you and your father's family will perish. And who knows but that you have come to your royal position for such a time as this?"* (Esther 4:14)

If she didn't try to do something, her family would be killed. You know Mordecai was like, "Girl, you better get your head straight. God put you in this position because He knew what was going to happen, and you're the one He chose to save His people." Mordecai also threw in that last statement, which has so much meaning. God knows *all* things, and He'd been preparing Esther for this moment her entire life. It was her time to shine for God. He placed her in this position for *"such a time as this."*

I love Esther's response to Mordecai. She told him to gather all the Jews in Susa and fast for three days – no food or water. After those three days, she would approach the king, and if she dies, she dies (v. 15-16). What a brave woman. She accepted her fate. She didn't go and cry or throw up her hands and say "Nope, not gonna do it!" She took the matter straight to God. I can only imagine the fear she had, but it didn't stop her. After three days of fasting, she dressed in her royal robes and went to the inner court. The king saw her and held out his gold scepter. Whew! She escaped this round of death.

The king asked Esther what she wanted and told her he would give her up to half the kingdom. Esther didn't blurt out that she was Jewish, or that Haman was plotting to kill the Jews. Instead, she set up a series of different banquets, asking that Haman attend each of them. The king granted her wish. Haman was overjoyed that he was being singled out by the queen, but he was still angry that Mordecai would not kneel or show any fear when Haman came near him. He went home that evening and after bragging to his wife and friends about his wonderful day, he told them he was angry at Mordecai. They told him to set up a pole and ask the king to have Mordecai impaled on it. Haman thought it was a great idea and went to bed a happy man that evening.

And now for the plot twist. The book of Esther is only one out of two books in the Bible that doesn't mention God, but it's evident that He's very much a part of this story. King Xerxes couldn't sleep that night, and he asked someone to bring his book of chronicles and read it to him. This book is a record of all that has happened during his reign.

There was a story in the record about Mordecai exposing two of the king's officers that were plotting to kill him. An investigation was done, and it was found to be true, so the king had the two men executed. The king decided he wanted Mordecai to be honored. The next morning, he asks Haman:

"What should be done for the man the king delights to honor?"
(Esther 6:6)

Haman, thought the king was talking about him, so he told the king:

"This man should be wrapped in a royal robe that the king has worn and a horse that the king has ridden, and someone should lead him through the city streets telling everyone the king delights in this man." (Esther 6:7-9)

The king agreed. Mic drop. I wish I could have seen his face when he told Haman to do all those things for Mordecai.

Haman was like, "What!?" He couldn't believe it, but he did as the king ordered. He went home that evening and whined to his wife and friends about the horrible day he'd had. This was a sign that things weren't going to turn out well for Haman.

That same evening, Haman was at Queen Esther's banquet, and the king asked again what her request was. He reminded her that he would give her up to half the kingdom. She told the king plainly that her and her people were to be killed. The king was furious and demanded to know who would do such a thing. She pointed to Haman.

Oh boy! I wouldn't want to be Haman. The king was enraged and left to get one of his officers. While he was gone, Haman begged the queen for his life. When King Xerxes came back, he saw Haman fall all over Queen Esther, and he became even more enraged. One of the king's officers told him that Haman had set up a pole near his house, and that Haman was going to use it for Mordecai. So the king had Haman impaled on that same pole. Wow. Our God is a just God – you don't mess with what's His.

The king then signed over Haman's estate to Esther. He gave Mordecai the job Haman had. He told Esther to write a decree and send it to all the king's provinces declaring they put a stop to the annihilation of the Jews. What a story!

The book of Esther is another great example of God's people *standing on faith together.* He heard their cries in heaven and showed up in a mighty, magnificent way! They prayed *in* faith, stood *on* faith, and believed together *in* faith that God would take care of them. We have the same capability to do what this group of people did thousands of years ago. God can turn our greatest sorrows into joy – all it requires is faith.

The Good Stuff

What if faith spread around the world like coronavirus? Imagine what that would look and feel like for a moment. Faith comes with all the things of God – His grace, mercy, and healing. It would also come with all the fruits of the Spirit: love, joy, peace, forbearance, kindness, goodness, faithfulness, gentleness, and self-control (Gal. 5:22-23).

What if that swept all over the world, and the media began to report all the good things that would come from such a movement? The evil would be revealed in all the dark corners of the earth. Darkness would be turned to light. Lies would be exposed, and truths would be revealed. Depression, mental illness, bipolar disorder – all the things that torment our minds, would be gone. Sickness in our bodies would be healed through our faith. Hate, anger, pain, rejection, and division would no longer exist – only unity. Wouldn't that be wonderful? And is it even possible? (More on this topic later.)

Where are we starting? You don't have to look far to see there are still some really good people in our world. During the coronavirus pandemic, an anonymous donor bought three different $50 gift cards from restaurants in Des Moines, Iowa for every single resident that lived there. This added up to more than $82,000. The donor had someone contact the mayor and together, all the details were worked out. Every single household received three $50 gift cards to three different restaurants.[3] This not only blessed the residents, but also the restaurants that were struggling to stay open. That is a double blessing!

Some of our healthcare workers were exhausted during the pandemic, and several videos surfaced on social media of people who parked their cars all around hospitals to play worship songs over the facilities. People held signs up that let the healthcare workers know they were praying for them, they were loved, and they were appreciated. One video captured some of the nurses and doctors standing on top of the hospital building worshipping and praying along with the people in their cars. It was beautiful to watch. The body of Christ was unified in their appreciation for all the hard work our healthcare workers were putting in.[456] They used their faith to stand together during a pandemic.

There are many more stories just like these. Many of the elderly, who were more at risk to this virus, feared to leave their homes to get food and supplies. It became a mission in some communities to take care of the ones that couldn't do it themselves. People took to apps like "Next Door" to find out the needs of their neighbors and try to meet the demands. Food drives popped up in many cities offering bags or boxes of free groceries for families in need. Churches did drive-through food pantries for the needy. Masks became a hot commodity, and many people were sewing them as fast as they could, then giving them away to essential workers that were exposed to the virus every day.

God was always working, always guiding, and directing His children. Sometimes it is hard to find the good stuff in the middle of a trial or tribulation, but it is there. During the hard times, God may ask you to do something you've never done before. It could mean that just like Esther, it's your time to shine. Are you ready to serve?

Is it Possible?

During the coronavirus pandemic, it was difficult to not get caught up in all the scary numbers and stories on the news. Fear is a strong emotion that can take over every part of our life, and we simply can't live that way. If we didn't have faith, fear would win. God doesn't want any of us to live in fear. He knows that fear plays a huge factor in our daily lives, so he placed the words "fear not" in the Bible three hundred and sixty-five times – one for each day of the year.

A few of my favorite verses are:

"Fear not, for I am with you." (NKJV Isaiah 41:10)

"Do not be afraid; do not be discouraged, for the Lord your God will be with you wherever you go." (NIV Joshua 1:9)

"For God has not given us a spirit of fear, but of power and of love and of a sound mind." (NKJV 2 Timothy 1:7).

Choose faith over fear. God will give you the courage and strength you need to overcome your deepest fears. There is nothing that could ever compare to the goodness of God. It doesn't matter what you're going through, because God already has the answer.

As Christians, we know that Jesus is coming back soon. The Bible tells us that people will call evil good and good evil (Isa. 5:20). The devil is angry because he knows his time is short here on earth. My mind can't even wrap around some of the evil stories I've heard during my lifetime. They are horrid and heartbreaking. This evil will continue until Jesus comes back and sends the devil to the lake of fire. My children, grandchildren, great grandchildren, and so forth will continue to see the evil that is among us here on earth. And although none of us know the day or hour Jesus will return, there is no doubt in my heart that He is coming soon.

So, back to the good stuff I mentioned earlier. What if we could spread faith and the good things of God here on earth just as the coronavirus spread around the world? Is it possible to make that kind of impact on the ones that are lost? Is it possible to spread faith, hope, and love globally? And if it's possible, how would we be able to take on this monumental task?

Brothers and sisters in Christ, I want to encourage you today that it's possible to do all of that, and more! We are the body of Christ.

I've said this many times throughout this book. We are in unity with God, Jesus, and the Holy Spirit. He will guide and direct us, but we must have faith, and we must do it together. *Standing on faith together* will be a *movement* unlike anything we've ever seen or experienced before. God is calling each of us to unify with the body of Christ, which means it's time for us to jump on board so we don't get left behind. Amen!

What impossible situation are you currently in? The one that you've been in for a while, but you don't think there is any way to possibly get out of it. Write it down. Be prepared for miracles to happen as soon as your fellow Christians begin to pray for you. The first step is to display an act of faith – trust that God will help you.

Revival

We've seen and heard about revivals breaking out all around the world. According to Dictionary.com, a revival is defined as "an awakening in a church community; an evangelistic service or a series of services for the purpose of effecting a religious awakening." We need a global faith revival! One like we've never experienced before.

When I was twenty-six years old, I attended contemporary Christian singer Carman's concert at Texas Stadium in Irving, Texas. I was mesmerized by the presence of God at that concert. Revival broke out in that stadium, and I stood in awe as many people came to know Christ that day. Over seventy thousand people attended that concert, and I know they were touched deeply by the Holy Spirit. It's my one and only experience of a revival with that many people, and it's a cherished memory.

As a Christian, I've felt the rumbling in my spirit for some time now. God is up to something, and it involves every single one of us here on earth – saved or not saved. I don't want to be left behind. So, the only thing I know to do is this: pray, seek God, and have faith. I trust that God will place me in the perfect position at the perfect time to do what

He's called me to do. I have faith that He will do the same for you and all of His children.

As we stand on faith together for the glory of God, I believe a revival will break out that will touch millions of people. That's how big my faith is, and it's only a tiny reflection of how big our God is.

Do you want to be a part of what God is doing? I want to share with the world that Christians are uniting in faith – they are not alone. We are *standing on faith together,* and we will no longer be silent. Amen!

CHAPTER 6: BEAUTY IN UNITY

What do you feel God was saying to you during the time you were quarantined? What is it going to take for you to accomplish what He showed you?

What impossible situation are you currently in? The one that you've been in for a while, but you don't think there is any way to possibly get out of it.

Do you want to be a part of what God is doing?

CHAPTER 7

From Division to Unity

Are you the person that gives up if you don't get something you really want? Or are you the person that is persistent sometimes to the point where you irritate others because of it? I'm more of the persistent type, but I've been at the point many times when I just wanted to give up. My husband knows more than anyone else that I'm persistent. If I'm not satisfied with something that we're discussing – wait, okay – arguing about, he knows that I won't stop pestering him until the issue has been resolved. I'm a firm believer that after faith in God, communication is the key to a happy marriage. Persistence has never failed me.

Jesus tells us not to give up. In Luke 18:1-5, He tells His disciples a parable about a judge that didn't care about God or what other people thought. He explains that a widow kept coming to the judge asking for justice against her adversary. Jesus tells us that the judge wasn't a caring person, so why would he care about some widow that had an issue with someone else? Because he didn't care about the widow, he refused to help her. But the widow was persistent – she didn't give up. She kept coming to the judge with her plea.

I can picture the judge's face when he saw the widow come to him day after day. I'm sure he rolled his eyes and thought to himself, *here she is again! Why can't she just get over it and move on?* I can also picture the widow's face every time she walked into the judge's presence. She had a determined look and thought, *I'm not giving up until he delivers the justice I've been asking for! I'll bother him every single day if that's what it takes!*

Sure enough, the judge got sick of her pestering him, so he tells himself that since the widow won't leave him alone, he'll see that she gets justice. The widow's persistence pays off, and justice is served.

Jesus tells the disciples in verses 6-8:

"listen to what the unjust judge says. And will not God bring about justice for his chosen ones, who cry out to him day and night? Will he keep putting them off? I tell you, he will see that they get justice, and quickly."

We must be diligent in our persistence. We must never give up. God hears, and He answers. He dishes out perfect justice to those who are doing evil.

Remember that God doesn't always answer our prayers the way we want them to be answered. He may answer your prayer in a way you don't expect. He'll provide manna in the form of coriander seed, and in order to make bread, the seed must be grinded. It required work for the Israelites to get what they prayed so desperately for. But God provided exactly what they needed, and we must trust that He'll do the same for each of us.

There is another sentence at the end of Luke 18, verse 8 that I want to share with you. It gave me great pause when I read it, because it's profound. Jesus said:

"However, when the Son of Man comes, will he find faith on the earth?"

The word *however* is a contrast word that is used to contradict what was previously said. After thinking about it, I read the parable again. The widow is seeking justice; the judge denies it multiple times; the widow doesn't give up; the judge finally grants her justice. Jesus tells us God will do the same for His chosen ones who persistently cry out to Him. God will see that His children get justice. *However,* when Jesus comes back, will He find faith here on earth?

Why would Jesus say that? Jesus knows the future, so He already knows there's a lack of faith here on earth. Picture the throne room in Heaven for a moment. God is sitting there listening to *all* the prayer requests that are coming from people on earth. Some of His people are joyful and praising Him for all the wonderful things He's done for them. Some are mourning for the loss of loved ones. Many are crying out to Him, desperately seeking answers to prayers. Others are whining, moaning, and complaining about things that aren't fair in life and demanding to know where God is in all the chaos. Many others don't even care about God, and they're living their life as if they don't know that Hell actually is a place. He sees and hears all His children. As these prayer requests reach God, He sends His angels by the thousands to answer them. God is constantly working to help His children. There are so many prayers He's answered that we never even give Him credit for. Many other times, He's helped us, and it wasn't even something we asked or prayed for. He loves us so, so much, but we still don't get who He is to each one of us. So, in the parable above, Jesus gives us an example of a woman pestering the judge with her request until the judge finally helps her. He then tells His disciples that God will do the same for the ones who cry out to Him. God answers our prayers, yet we don't have faith.

Do you have a story similar to the one from Luke 18? Were you persistent to the point of annoyance? And did something change? Someone is going through something right now, and even though they are persistent, they are growing tired and weary. We need to encourage our Christian family to keep the faith because we are standing with them.

Christians, I'm asking you to go deeper in your faith. Search your hearts and ask your Heavenly Father what you can do to help others find the deep, abiding faith God is looking for. When God thinks about you, does He have any doubts about your faith in Him? Faith in God is the most important weapon you'll ever carry, because through that faith, you have the power and authority of God and all His angels standing with you to face the enemy that wants to destroy you and your family. I promise you that you will not lose. Have faith and stand on it. Your victory awaits!

The Silent Majority

After reading this book, my hope and prayer is that you understand how important your faith is to God. Stay connected to the tree of living water. We are with you, fighting the same enemy, and together we can and will defeat him. We are the silent majority here on earth. We don't proclaim hatred or division. We kneel and pray. We don't destroy things or hurt people. We silently weep for the destruction that continues to get worse. We fight together; we stand on faith together. We are one with God – the body of Christ, and we already have the victory. As shocking as things are and continue to turn for the worse, we shouldn't be surprised because Jesus told us over two thousand years ago that these things would happen. As I said in the previous chapter, we need revival. We need an awakening for God's people to turn from their sin before it's too late.

A deep pruning is taking place. God is exposing the ones that are evil, and He's asking for His chosen ones to stand up and fight the enemy of our soul. We can no longer be silent. We must roar loudly like a lion so the enemy hears us. As we are standing on faith together, praying in unity, our voices are lifted up to God in Heaven, and his angels will come fight the battle for us. We won't have to use physical weapons. We will defeat the devil with the words we speak, our faith, and our unity.

God wants each of us to produce the good fruits of the Spirit listed in Galatians 5:22. Remember, for the ones that aren't producing good fruit, He will decide if they are to be cut away. He'll continue to prune the branches that bear good fruit, so we don't get lost along the way and end up being one of the dead branches that He cuts off permanently.

I encourage you to stay strong. God will bring you through whatever you're going through. Trust in Him. Trust in the process.

As the silent majority, my prayer is we listen to what God is saying to us. When we stand together in faith, He's listening – He hears our cries.

Lord, please help us. There are so many who are lost, and they have never experienced Your love. Help me show them Your glory. Just a drop of Your love will change someone's entire life. Allow us to be Your hands and feet. We need unity. Help us get to the place that nothing else matters but You, Lord. I pray these words silently to You, but my heart wants to shout them from the rooftop. You deserve praise from every living thing here on earth. I pray for a revival and awakening to break out that shatters all previous records… one that sweeps around the entire world. I pray that your chosen ones stand on faith together, and as we are unified in faith, that You would release Your power, love, peace, hope, grace, mercy, healing, salvation, transformation, restoration, knowledge, truth, wisdom, and everything else that comes from You. Oh God, hear my prayer. In Your mighty name I pray, amen!

When you pray, listen for His voice. It's there in the quiet places within your heart, mind, body, and soul. Yes, we are the silent majority, but we have the power of God Almighty. Through Him miracles will be released, lives will be changed, and people will be saved. All it takes is faith as small as a mustard seed.

What Does God Want from You?

Have you ever asked God what He wants from you? Or maybe you've asked why He created you? I'll be the first to admit I've asked both of those questions. When I first became a Christian, I knew I was different because I felt different. The old me was gone, and the new me was just beginning (2 Cor. 5:17). I was excited, but I didn't have a clue how much my life was going to change. I was eager to learn all I could, not knowing or understanding that the devil wanted to destroy this newfound love I'd found with Jesus. Doubt, worry, and fear were planted deeply in my everyday life. But I also had that seed of faith that was slowly growing, and doubt, worry, and fear were uprooted from the depths of my heart and tossed away.

I prayed every single day for God to show me what He wanted from me. His answer was always the same. "Have faith." That's it – two simple words. *Have faith.* I heard those words hundreds, if not thousands, of times, but I didn't understand how or why that was all God wanted from me. So, as a person that is persistent to the point of being annoying, I kept asking Him, hoping He would change His answer. He didn't. I argued this point with God many times, but He never gave me what I thought I wanted to hear. I'm good at over-complicating things; God knows this about me, so He gave me those two words – Have faith. I eventually accepted His words and embraced them with my whole being. Because my purpose is to have faith, it has been tested multiple times over, and I've learned so much through His refining fire.

Do you know how silver is refined? According to *Webster's New World Dictionary*, refine means "to free from impurities." To refine a piece of silver, a silversmith holds it over the hottest part of the fire so it will burn all the impurities away. The silversmith sits and watches until it's complete. If he leaves it in the fire too long, the silver will be destroyed. He knows it is fully refined when he can see his image in it.[7] Wow! What a revelation.

God does the same for us. He never leaves our side. He is always watching, and He knows the exact time to pull us from the fire, or what we call trials and tribulations. When we are going through the worst moments in life, God is melting all our impurities away. And when He finally sees Himself reflected in us, He pulls us away from the fire. We are set free from sin and the chains that are holding us down. We are purified, cleansed, and made whole.

What is the thing that you've felt in your spirit that God has been speaking over you? It may not be the same as mine. Is He calling you to be a Pastor? Or a counselor? Maybe He's calling you to simply love others. Whatever it is, I promise you this – if He's spoken it over you, it's your destiny. Step into it, embrace it, and run with it. God will take you on a journey that you'll never regret. There are people out there that need what God has placed in you. What you have is a gift that no one else has. You're unique, special, talented, and a blessing to so many people that you haven't even met yet. With God on your side, you'll be unstoppable. Be persistent. Never give up. God will show you the way.

Don't Fear/Don't Panic

I've mentioned several times that fear is an effective tool the enemy uses to destroy what God wants for each of us. I encourage you to recognize your fears and give them to God. He will give you His peace and help you move forward. Fear has been a very strong factor throughout the pandemic. But there is also hope and unity that has taken place on a level I haven't seen in my lifetime. Throughout the pandemic, stories continue to flood in of all the good things people are doing for each other. Humanity still exists, and we need more kind, caring people to help the ones that need it. So, what happens when the pandemic is over? Are we going to go back to the way things were? It's a question many people are asking. The answer is: Nobody knows. The only thing any of us can do is pray and take it one day at a time. Only God knows what will take place, and that is where we need to place our faith and trust.

We shouldn't fear the unknown because to God, it's not unknown. He knows the past, present, and future. This is where our faith comes into play. If I have faith that God will take care of this big giant coronavirus, and trust that He's allowed it here for a very specific purpose, then I can focus on what He's called me to do. When I do this, I'm at peace, because I know that whatever happens, God already knows about it, and He's already there.

Don't fear what is in the complete control of God. If I listened to all the negativity about the coronavirus and how our government is even more divided because of it, I'd very quickly get caught up in the fear and division that is sweeping around the world. I'm not going to give the enemy what he desperately wants. Instead, I choose to focus on the positive things I've seen and heard about. The hands and feet of Jesus are all around me. God's light is shining in the darkness, and I believe this is just the beginning of what He's about to do here on earth.

If you're struggling with fear or doubt, take it to God. Remember who He is. He'll never leave or forsake you. He'll draw you into His light and chase all the bad things away. He has you in the crook of His arm. He won't allow anything to harm you. There is nothing the love of God can't fix. Keep your eyes on the things of God, and the panic that tries to take hold of you will cease. Psalm 1:1-3 says:

> *"Blessed is the one who does not walk in step with the wicked or stand in the way that sinners take or sit in the company of mockers, but whose delight is in the law of the Lord, and who meditates on his law day and night. That person is like a tree planted by streams of water, which yields its fruit in season and whose leaf does not wither – whatever they do prospers."*

Brothers and sisters in Christ, you're His, and you're loved and blessed beyond anything you can think or imagine.

Going from Division to Unity

> *"I appeal to you, brothers and sisters, in the name of our Lord Jesus Christ, that all of you agree with one another in what you say and that there be no divisions among you, but that you be perfectly united in mind and thought."* (1 Cor. 1:10)

> *"How good and pleasant it is when God's people live together in unity."* (Psalm 133:1)

Division comes in different forms. It comes at us through our marriage, family, friends, work environment, and our government. Division destroys us from within. It gives us feelings of hatred, anger, frustration, and bitterness. Division causes destruction. It slowly destroys everything that we've worked so hard to achieve. We know from John 10:10 that the devil's job is to steal, kill, and destroy all those who oppose him. He's done a good job wreaking havoc here on earth. We are more divided than ever before. It's easy to judge people like this, because we know it's wrong. But let's be honest – we're all guilty of doing something wrong during our lifetime. I know I'm not perfect, even as a Christian – I still make mistakes. I know God loves me, and I humbly ask for His forgiveness and try to do better.

Jesus suffered for the sins of every person here on earth. Just as my sins are forgiven because of Jesus, I also must forgive those who sin against me. Faith has helped me do this. I gave all my heart to God when I became a Christian, and it completely changed my life. If God can do this for me, He can do it for anyone. I now look at people through God's eyes. If they've hurt someone, it means they're probably hurting. People aren't cruel just because they feel like it. Something has happened to them along their life journey that molds them into the person they are. These people need Jesus, just as you and I do. God doesn't want any one of us to suffer, but so many continue to turn away from Him. They believe the lies of the devil, which causes even more division. We can't continue this way forever – destruction is upon us, and we can do something about it.

So how do we go from division to unity? We need to be unified as the body of Christ like we never have before. God is calling us to unite because there is power in unity. Jesus tells us that if two or more people are gathered together, He is with us, and if we're in unity on what we're asking for, God will take care of it (Matt. 18:19-20). We *stand on faith together* in unity, and we pray for division to leave our marriage, family, friends, government, and our country, and every country around the world. We believe, in faith, that God will hear our cries in Heaven, and

He'll move mountains for us. We stand for peace, not division. We stand for joy and love, not hate. We stand for healing, not brokenness. We stand on faith together and watch as God does exactly as He's promised.

I mentioned the scripture below earlier in this book, but it's worth repeating again.

"If my people, who are called by my name, will humble themselves and pray and seek my face and turn from their wicked ways, then I will hear from heaven, and I will forgive their sin and will heal their land." (2 Chron. 7:14)

It's not too late; we can still make a difference. We can show Jesus that He will find faith on earth when He returns. All you need to do is watch the news if you want to see and hear the negative things going on in our world. My hopes and prayers are that we turn people towards God so He can heal their hearts and minds. Brothers and sisters, let's start a movement and a revival that will change millions of lives. Let's stand on faith together and pray for unity over division. Amen!

Let's start talking about a revival. Where will it be held? When will it happen? How can we all gather together and pray in faith? We need to take back what the enemy has stolen from us. We can do this all around the world. We need to repent and ask God to forgive our sins. Let's set the enemy on his heels, so he can tuck his tail and flee. God will make a way when there seems to be no way – all we need to do is ask Him. We can do this, so let's make it happen. I'm ready! Will you join me?

Expect Miracles

I want to leave you with one last story from the Bible. It's in the book of Joshua. After Moses died, Joshua was placed in charge of the Israelites. The first task he was assigned was to cross over the Jordan River so they could take possession of the land that was promised by God. God told Joshua to be strong and courageous. Those are words spoken only when something's about to happen that requires strength and courage. Not only did they have to cross over to the other side of the river, they also knew they would have to fight to get the land God promised them. They would need both strength and courage.

The Jordan River is up to thirteen hundred feet deep, so it wouldn't be an easy task getting everyone to the other side. After camping by the river for three days, Joshua instructed the priests to take the ark of the covenant to the edge of the river. Once the priest's feet touched the water, the Jordan parted just like the Red Sea did for Moses. Once all the Israelites crossed safely to the other side, the water returned to its normal state. This news spread around to nearby cities, and people were terrified of the Israelites. God had a plan, and everything He was doing was working in favor of the Israelites.

Their next stop was the city of Jericho. Once they arrived at Jericho, they discovered a wall that surrounded the entire city. I'm sure Joshua was thinking, *how are we supposed to take possession of a city that has a wall around it?* Joshua didn't have to wait long to find out. He received instructions from God to have his army march around the city once a day for six days. While they were marching, they were instructed to play their trumpets, and the priests were to follow them carrying the ark of the covenant.

On the seventh day, the soldiers were to march around Jericho seven times. Doesn't that seem like an odd request from God? But Joshua didn't question the command; he simply obeyed and so did his entire army. They were in complete unity with one another. On that final day, after they had marched around Jericho seven times, Joshua commanded his soldiers to shout because the Lord had given them the city. His soldiers shouted with a roar, and the wall surrounding Jericho fell to the ground. Wow! I can imagine the sound of that roar had to be deafening. Once the wall fell, the soldiers entered the city and took possession of it.

This is an amazing story, but I want to pause here and think about *how* these miraculous things happened. We know God performed the miracles, but the Israelites played a very big role in what God was doing. At the beginning of Joshua chapter one, after God tells Joshua to cross the Jordan River to claim the land He promised them, Joshua gave a great speech to encourage the people. This is their response:

"Then they answered Joshua, 'Whatever you have commanded us we will do, and wherever you send us we will go. Just as we fully obeyed Moses, so we will obey you. Only may the Lord God be with you as he was with Moses. Whoever rebels against your word and does not obey it, whatever you may command them, will be put to death. Only be strong and courageous.'" (Joshua 1:16-18)

Joshua listened and obeyed everything that God asked him to do. He relayed this information to the Israelites, and they also obeyed everything God asked of them. They were in perfect unity together. This unity allowed God to come in and remove every obstacle that stood in the way of what He promised them. I know in my spirit that He will do the same for us today.

This is perfect for the revival I mentioned earlier. I keep getting a vision of the body of Christ shouting, roaring like a lion – our voices harmoniously coming together – and the sound is beautiful! God hears, He sees, He already knows what needs to be done, He's just waiting on us to come boldly to Him – without fear – and He will answer our prayers. Can you picture it? God is so good!

Can we start a community of believers that are willing to stand on faith together for every single thing God asks of us? You bet we can! As we unite, God will give us direction on what He wants us to do, just as He did the soldiers in the Israelite army. When Jesus comes back, I believe He will find faith here on earth. I believe God is waiting for us to unite together so a revival will break out that will be unlike any revival there ever has been. When we stand together, God is there. Miracles will take place all around us, just like the walls of Jericho collapsed many years ago. Expect to be in awe of what He's about to do here on earth.

Together

Standing on faith is something I've done since I came to know Jesus. It's the together part that stumps me. This is me being real. I'm not a bold person, and I've experienced the pain of rejection many times in my life. These past few months in quarantine have made me realize that I can't sit quietly in my home and pray for this message to spread around the world. I know what God has asked of me, and now I must put my fears aside and boldly *stand on faith together* with Christians all around the world.

Remember earlier when I stated that we're the silent majority? That is true, but we need to find our voice. We need to speak boldly of the things God has placed in our hearts. I believe we can do this together. We can encourage each other through it. God is asking for our obedience; He'll do the rest. I choose to obey what He's asking me to do, and I'll do it. I know not everyone will receive His message or care about it. But I also know that there are people out there that need this, and that is the reason I wrote this book.

Yes, we're living in scary times. Who knows what's going to happen with the coronavirus? So many of us are questioning what to believe from all the different news reports. Is the coronavirus as bad as they say it is? How much longer do we have to wear a mask? When will schools be fully open again? When they come up with a vaccine, are we all going to be forced to get it? What about the economy? Is our government ever going to be unified instead of divided? Why is this virus so political? The list of questions could go on and on. Know this – God isn't surprised by any of it, and He holds all the answers we're seeking.

How do we stand on faith together in a post pandemic world? We boldly come together as the body of Christ. We face our fears and trust that God will do for us just as He did for the Israelites many years ago. I don't know if things will ever be the same, and maybe that's a good thing. What I do know is we serve a mighty God that isn't scared of anything. We need change, we need Jesus, and we need to stand together so God can show us the power *we* have through our faith and obedience to Him. He's ready to show all of us exactly what He's capable of. If I were the devil, I'd be shaking in my boots. Amen.

It's time for us to stand on faith together and change our world. We need to boldly come together and seek God for the answers needed to heal our world. In faith, in unity – together – we will change the world. I ask you to join me on this journey. Will you stand with me?

"For in Christ Jesus neither circumcision nor uncircumcision has any value. The only thing that counts is faith expressing itself through love." (Galatians. 5:6)

NOTES

Sources

Chapter 5: Beauty in Unity

1. Lee, Alicia. "A Facebook Group Matches RVs That Are Sitting Idle with Health Care Workers Who Need a Place to Isolate after Long Hospital Shifts." 01 Apr. 2020. Web. 07 Sept. 2020.

2. LeBlanc, Sarah Kay. "Anonymous Donor Sends $150 in Gift Cards to Every Household in 1,400-person Iowa Town." *USA Today*. Gannett Satellite Information Network, 08 Apr. 2020. Web. 07 Sept. 2020. <https://www.usatoday.com/story/news/nation/2020/04/06/anonymous-donor-sends-150-gift-cards-every-household-iowa-town/2953328001/>.

3. Corbley, McKinley. "Mystery Mom Has Been Leaving Out Free Bagged Lunches 'Made With Love' for Anyone Who May Need Them." *Good News Network*. 07 Apr. 2020. Web. 07 Sept. 2020. <https://www.goodnewsnetwork.org/mystery-mom-leaves-out-free-bagged-lunches-during-covid19-shutdowns/>.

4. Gavan, Hillary. "Worshippers Sing in Honor of Healthcare Workers." *Beloit Daily News*. 31 Mar. 2020. Web. 07 Sept. 2020. <https://www.beloitdailynews.com/news/covid-19/worshippers-sing-in-honor-of-healthcare-workers/article_b5ae72dc-a5bb-5699-8dfb-38908a271d70.html>.

5. Murphy, Monica. "People Gathered outside Goshen Hospital to Pray for Health Care Workers." *Https://www.wndu.com*. 02 Apr. 2020. Web. 07 Sept. 2020. <https://www.wndu.com/content/news/People-pray-and-worship-outside-Goshen-Hospital-to--569340171.html>.

6. Nagus, Chris. "Locals Take Worship to Hospital Parking Lots: 'This Is Bigger than All of Us'." *KMOV.com*. 01 Apr. 2020. Web. 07 Sept. 2020. <https://www.kmov.com/news/locals-take-worship-to-hospital-parking-lots-this-is-bigger-than-all-of-us/article_1ba99f04-7482-11ea-94cf-7bd229d077ec.html>.

Chapter 7: From Division to Unity

1. Goodwin, J. (2019, April 27). The Refiner's Fire - a lesson from the process of refining fire in our lives. Retrieved September 08, 2020, from https://ourgoodwinjourney.com/refining-fire/

Acknowledgements

My deepest appreciation to everyone that joined my Good Talk Launch Team. The message in this book is deeply personal for me, and I'm thankful to each of you for joining with me to help get the message out to our world.

Katrina Zacca, Kaitlyn Beck, Robin Moore, Meagan Miller, Sissy Morgan, Breanna Zacca, Daniel Zacca, Tracey Perez, Suni Gail, Kelli Gilby, Jan Ward, Susan Thompson, Kim Moore, Jorja Brown, Denise Turner, Cyndi Scott, Chanel Hargrove, Pamela Austin, Patrick Benton, Debbie Moore, Karen R. Gibson, H.L. Laffoon, Nelson Argueta, Tonya B. Evans, Tammy Fuller, Jackie S. Alvarado, Marjay Cooper, Riley Zacca, Wanda Ervin, Frances Bishop, Tanya Moore, Marc Moore, Jane Smith, Nelson Webb, Michelle McGough, Mary Flowers, Frank Mushinski, Dawn Brewster, AnneMarie Flaherty, Mayra Herrera, Michael Roos, JoDella Sickles, Mike Gibson, Elizabeth Olson, Melinda Hibdon, Bobbie M. Burkett, Shelly C. Horton, Bonnie S. Gardner, Christyne H. Meager, Lisa Liberato, Sarah E. Smith, Ed Cluff, Sandra Cluff, Bryan Hilliard, Paula L. McKenzie, Sallie Workman, Maggie Vaught, Claudia T. Serrano, Jessica Hardee, Lisa G. Beaty, Barbara Beebe, Loyda Ebacher, Megan Bee, Robin Pedrero, and Lauri M. Bauman

Acknowledgments

A special thank you to my husband, Shaun. I never imagined when we got married thirty-five years ago that I could love you any more than I did that day – but I do – I love you even more today. Thank you for all that you do for our family. You work hard to take care of us, and I deeply appreciate you. You are my everything, and I'm the happiest when you are by my side.

To my children: Daniel and his wife, Breanna, Katrina, Kaitlyn and her husband, Chance, I love each of you so very much, and I'm thankful for all that you bring to my life. Never give up on your dreams because each of you deserve the best of everything. Thank you for your encouragement in all that I do – it means more than you'll ever know. I am so proud of all that each of you have accomplished. You and my grandchildren are my greatest blessings.

I also want to give a BIG thank you to Leticia Herrera. Your art is beautiful and inspiring. Thank you for putting together the perfect piece of art for the cover of this book. It took my breath away when I first laid my eyes on it. Thank you so much for allowing me to use it for my book cover. I absolutely love it!

If you are interested in Letitia's art, please go to her website: letitiaherreraart.com.

I want to give a very special thank you to Robin Moore. I've never met anyone so dedicated to helping others become who God's called them to be. You have such a compelling gift, and I'm grateful you allowed me into your life. You not only taught me how to be a better writer, but you also taught me to be more courageous – and that, my friend, has changed my entire world. Thank you, Robin, for being who you are – a magnificent talented artist, best-selling author, developmental editor, friend, and a uniquely special human being. You are simply the best.

Robin is the best-selling author of several books, including: *#NOFILTERNEEDED: Shortcuts to Becoming an Influencer, Maverick Wisdom from King Solomon's Proverbs, Mentored by a Maverick,* and a children's book series about a pound-dog dachshund who finds his forever family in *No Chicken for Joe.* One of her many talents is a developmental editor. I highly recommend her if you are interested in writing a book. You can reach Robin through her website: robinkmoore.com.

My final thank you is to God Almighty. I'm so thankful for Your persistence in pushing me to go deeper in my faith. We've had many good, long talks about this book, and I'll cherish those moments forever. My prayer every single day is for You to prepare the hearts and minds of every single person here on earth for The Great Awakening that is about to sweep the entire world. Save us, Lord. Show your children how much You love them. Help the ones You've called for this purpose to bring your children back to You. Let us not grow weary in the task You've set before us. We are stronger *together* – let us never forget that.

I didn't think any of what I've accomplished was even possible – but I did it – because of You. I love You more than anything, and I'll be forever thankful and grateful for all that You've done for me and my family.

STANDING ON FAITH TOGETHER IN A POST PANDEMIC WORLD

Thank you for purchasing my book *Standing on Faith Together in a Post Pandemic World.*

I would be greatly blessed if you would submit a review on the Amazon purchase page of this book.

You may add your name to my book launch list on my Facebook Page: Kathy Zacca for a chance to be featured in the acknowledgments of my next book due out soon!

AUTHOR BIO

Kathy Zacca has been a Secretary, Payroll Specialist, Office Manager, Customer Service Representative, and a Teacher at a private school. She is now doing what she loves most – writing! She and her husband, Shaun, live in Texas, where they raised their four children.

Kathy loves cooking for her family, and her favorite hobbies are cross stitching and reading. She also loves to travel. Her passion for writing comes from reading many different books from her childhood to adulthood. She loves how words on a page can be so inspiring and life changing, or how they can take you to a different world.

You can connect with Kathy on her website: KathyZacca.com.